Juan —
to the dancer!

JMulenny
♡

Jingle Bell Disorder

the doing, the undoing and the overdoing of Christmas

Jean-Marie Denning

BALBOA
PRESS
A DIVISION OF HAY HOUSE

Copyright © 2014 Jean-Marie Denning.

All rights reserved. No part of this book may be used or reproduced by any means, graphic, electronic, or mechanical, including photocopying, recording, taping or by any information storage retrieval system without the written permission of the publisher except in the case of brief quotations embodied in critical articles and reviews.

Balboa Press books may be ordered through booksellers or by contacting:

Balboa Press
A Division of Hay House
1663 Liberty Drive
Bloomington, IN 47403
www.balboapress.com
1 (877) 407-4847

Because of the dynamic nature of the Internet, any web addresses or links contained in this book may have changed since publication and may no longer be valid. The views expressed in this work are solely those of the author and do not necessarily reflect the views of the publisher, and the publisher hereby disclaims any responsibility for them.

The author of this book does not dispense medical advice or prescribe the use of any technique as a form of treatment for physical, emotional, or medical problems without the advice of a physician, either directly or indirectly. The intent of the author is only to offer information of a general nature to help you in your quest for emotional and spiritual well-being. In the event you use any of the information in this book for yourself, which is your constitutional right, the author and the publisher assume no responsibility for your actions.

Any people depicted in stock imagery provided by Thinkstock are models, and such images are being used for illustrative purposes only.
Certain stock imagery © Thinkstock.

Scripture quotations contained herein are from *The Holy Bible, Revised Standard Version, Catholic Edition*, copyright ©1952 [2nd edition, 1971] by the Division of Christian Education of the National Council of the Churches of Christ in the United States of America. Used by permission. All rights reserved.

Print information available on the last page.

ISBN: 978-1-4525-9780-5 (sc)
ISBN: 978-1-4525-9782-9 (hc)
ISBN: 978-1-4525-9781-2 (e)

Library of Congress Control Number: 2014920039

Balboa Press rev. date: 11/10/2017

To Viola

____a life full of jingle and joy!

Contents

Acknowledgements..ix
Preface xi
Introduction...xvii

Part 1: Opening

Jingle Bell Disorder (JBD)..1
The Gift of Memories: Remembering, Celebrating, Believing..........9
The Gift of Forgiveness: Bringing Forgiveness Home for the Holidays...19
The Gift of the Present..31
The Gift of Gratitude: It Is a Line to the Divine................43
The Gift of Giving: Giving, Receiving, Asking 53

Part 2: Maggie's Search for Christmas

Love Is a Toodle-Dee-Doo!..69
How to Get Your Jingle Back......................................83
Peace: No Assembly Required......................................95

Part 3: Closing

Jingle Bell Order (JBO)...113
Wrapping It Up 115
Bibliography..119

Acknowledgements

I would like to express a very special thank-you to my sons, John and Matthew. Your ongoing support is very much appreciated. Matt, thanks so much for helping me finish. Thank you, John for encouraging me to finish with you. You two are life's greatest gifts.

I would like to thank my family; especially Ruth (for many hours of helping me organize materials) and her daughter Lisa Lavoie for her illustrations. (Lalatopia) Thank you to Dot and Joe for sharing their resources and wisdom. Special thanks to my brothers Neil and Gary for ongoing support.

Friends are an essential part of anyone's life, and I would like to thank them for the special gift of encouragement, presence and support. Special thanks to Viola who lived life full of jingle and joy and demonstrated to me how to live life connected to spirit.

Thank you to all the people that contributed in some way in this process. I would like to extend a special thank you to; Wayne Curtis, Maggie McLaughlin, Anne Comeau, Leo Profit, Beth Armstrong, Terry Hayward, Chantal Ouellette, Vivian MacPhail, Rev. Dr. Norm Whitney, Bro.Matthew Chukwudi Onwugigbo, E. McCluskey, Richard Boileau, M.Boudreau, S.Wells, A.L.McCarthy, Karen Taylor, Lucie Desjardin, Sharon Cowan, Danna Mott, Terry and Gary Bartlett (for a total Christmas experience) Thanks for your encouragement and your patience.

Preface

> Unless you become like little children …
> —Jesus (Matthew 18:3)

Christmas is typically portrayed with a traditional, happy family sitting by the fireplace or at a perfectly set table. The twinkling reindeer on the roof with a cascade of Christmas decorations and the background Christmas music complete the picture. These images become imprinted on our hearts from an early age but do not necessarily correspond with our current experiences.

This lovely picture may appeal to some, but it appears to be out of sync with many, as the relentless call of the soul requests something more meaningful. There appears to be a deep-rooted desire in our humanity to create a life based on love for others and for self, along with a desire to connect to something greater than ourselves. There also seems to be a deep desire for validation, dignity, and respect, as well as an innate cry to sustain the beauty of our natural environment. At the very basis of each heartbeat there seems to be a need for things to make sense. If these elements are not present as a way of life, it is difficult to incorporate a sense of order in a celebration of Christmas.

There is no time like Christmas to experience the wild chase of the material world running counterintuitively to the intended values of the season. Even though we have long discovered that the material world does not satisfy the soul, the season seems to provide a sort of amnesia to this knowing. This amnesia sets up an underlying disconnect between our ideal Christmas and our actual Christmas experiences, which result in conflict between our day-to-day lives, and our soul-level needs. This book attempts to transform these disconnections by showing us how to discover the mystical elements that unite a life of spiritual integrity.

If we speak to police, social workers, or hospital staff, we might find a major disconnect between this ideal Christmas (for some) and what is actually going on for a significant part of the population. If we look at the stark reality of the poor, the unemployed, and the marginalized, we see a great distance between their reality and the reality portrayed by traditional Christmas hype. For many of us, regardless of our status and position, there is a gap between our ideal and actual Christmas experiences.

This book is about that gap. This gap, which often speaks to us through a longing, seems to be particularly strong during the holiday season. It is difficult to know what exactly to do with it. We know this longing is not about more money, more material things, or more food, for those who already have plenty. We seem to carry this longing in our hearts for something more meaningful, something happier and more sacred. We seem to long for sanity, simplicity, and spiritual connectedness.

The yearning in our hearts seems to request contact with a deeper order of things, one in which there is more fulfillment and harmony with unseen forces. Dr. Seuss said it best in How the Grinch Stole Christmas: "I puzzled and puzzled 'til my puzzler got sore—couldn't Christmas mean a little bit more?"

Jingle Bell Disorder (JBD) is a term used to describe the underlying dissonance that you might experience while riding the emotional roller coaster of Christmas. It aims to explore ways to integrate the multiple ups and downs of the ride. By addressing the backstories behind the roller-coaster ride of emotions at Christmas, as well as the paradoxes of the season, it is hoped that you will discover ways to live life daily connected to spirit.

This book, Jingle Bell Disorder, is a result of a personal exploration to find ways to make sense of the discrepancies between an actual and an ideal Christmas. The book's main aim is to explore these divergent aspects of the holiday experience so we each can live life daily connected to our spirit. During this personal journey, I have attempted to integrate the deepest spiritual longings with the conflicting secular demands of our times, combined with personal challenging circumstances.

Jingle Bell Disorder or the Christmas disconnect, is a difficult puzzle to solve because of a combination of factors, including consumer-based demands, deep-seated traditions and expectations, as well as the religious nature of the holiday. There are many contradictions regarding the internal and external conflicts within the Christmas season that call for some resolution.

As we delve further into this subject, it provides us with an opportunity to create a means of sifting through the contradictions and bringing together the pieces of the holiday that are in congruence with what we truly want at our deepest level. As we do this, the hope is to create a final picture that inspires us to discover ways to merge, blend, and soften the sacred into our daily lives. In so doing, it is hoped that we will find ways to move past what separates us so that we can create a life with more kindness, hope, and meaning. In this book, many pieces of the puzzle have been explored to help you complete your own puzzle.

Children completely understand the magic and beauty of Christmas. There is a mystical magic that speaks to a child's heart. As children, we enjoyed the magic of the lights, the silence, and the taste of grandma's apple pie. We remember these moments as adults. A child's magic has a sense that all is right in the world. The natural awe of a child can delight in playing outside in the snow, skating if ice was available, or building a castle with blocks. Christmas holds all the essential elements of a child's heart. The wide-open space provides a child with the experience of pure delight with the sounds, smells, and spirit of the holiday. As adults, our memories still hold all the joy and magic of this.

I Want to Become a Child Again

I want to be a child again at Christmas,
To taste the sweetness,
Smell the wonder,
And feel the magic.
I want to believe, in miracles and magnificence.
I want to reclaim my childlike ways,
Reclaim my innocence,
And jingle
And tingle with delight.

Looking back, it seems like Christmas was more of a magical place inside. It was a feeling of being fully alive. From this magical place it felt like I could do or be anything. The Christmas sights, sounds, and smells seemed to sparkle inside and out. Snow covered the resting hills which seemed to offer a mystical blanket of calm and delight.

The wood stove welcomed chilled hands and feet; it provided great meals as well as hot chocolate for total comfort. There was nothing that tasted better than breakfast on Christmas morning. A child's heart seems to synchronize with the rhythms of the earth and the heavens at Christmas.

Somehow, along the way, this magical place disappeared. The magic place felt iced over like a pond in winter. The outer chill of the winter seemed like it had shifted inside the soul. Nothing felt alive. The inside sparkle seemed to be replaced with an inner chill.

Something had gone wrong.

Instead of feeling connected to everything and everyone, there was an overwhelming sense of alienation, of being homesick even while being at home. It seemed like the spiritual world and the commercial world were duking it out for top spot. Between both of these worlds there was a childlike unending longing for more laughter, more fun, and more "chestnuts roasting on an open fire."

I was not aware how far I had ventured from my magical childhood ways until I received turkey-shaped pickle forks for Christmas. The gift, so unlike anything I would use or want, spoke about an urgent need for a complete change. It was not the first meaningless gift I had ever received, but somehow it was the one that rang a bell and declared it was time for more jingle.

This gift started a gradual thaw of the inside frozen terrain. The thaw occurred at different stages, somewhat like a turkey on Christmas Day. At first, I noticed only maxed-out credit cards, a fatigue that was unrelated but somehow connected, and an all-over body ache that would not go away. For the most part, I just wanted to throw out the turkey and order a pizza.

As I tried to make sense of it all, several faces drifted through my mind. It was as if these faces might lead me to more meaning or a deeper understanding. The faces, although different from each other, seemed almost relational to a quest for meaning.

The first person that came to my mind was a high school student's shadowed face after he had delivered Christmas packages to people without floors or stoves. I saw the face of a child with a parent spending Christmas in prison. I saw the face of a single mother who needed to choose between having a meal and having gifts for her children on Christmas Day.

As my mind drifted, I saw the face of the lady next door who was worried about which painting to buy her husband. Next was a man who had just purchased season tickets to the local sports team, as well as a trip to Disney for his family. I saw the face of the pastor as he spoke of God's abundant life for us as his church sat smack in the middle of apparent poverty.

What faces do you see when you think of Christmas?

A Journey to Jingle Bell Order (JBO)

Throughout this book, you are invited to journey from Jingle Bell Disorder (JBD) to an enchanted place of Jingle Bell Order (JBO). JBO has less to do with material things and more to do with the true riches of integrity, honesty, and restorative dialogue. It is home to those who wish to expand the global consciousness to one of peace, love, and joy. It is magical and mystical place where you can rekindle your childlike wonder. In JBO there is a sense of happiness, innocence, and fun.

It is my wish that we discover ways to integrate life's challenges and become one with the flow of life. On this journey there will be places to build a joyful, magical, childlike heart—regardless of your beliefs or status in life. As we travel to this inner terrain, we will be invited to leave the heaviness of life behind. Our final destination, JBO, is a place to experience the magic and miracles as a way of life, and here we learn to live heaven on earth.

Before any trip it is important to visualize and imagine. Imagination is the fuel of a child. So just for a second, close your eyes and imagine leaving all your command performances behind and arriving at a place that is total peace, which means total order. In JBO, everything sparkles with delight and flows with grace. In this place there is respect and reverence for all of life. Celebration is a way of life.

Everyone in JBO takes very good care of themselves. People take good care of one another and the environment. The welcome sign invites you to a place of kindness, safety, and respect for all things. In JBO, everyone offers his or her unique gifts and is able to receive the gifts of others. Every person shines with delight and dances with the wonder of each moment. Everyone belongs in this place. There is only joy and magical moments.

This is a book of creative nonfiction, inspired by truth, and a result of my imagination, as well as personal and collective narratives. The book aims to be an addition to any religion or belief system, in order to build harmony among all people. It does not represent any medical advice but aims to inspire wellness by building an inner sense of calm. Throughout the book there are narratives and backstories in which people's names have been changed or are fictitious.

I have presented ideas that I found helpful on my own journey, and I hope to point out things that will guide you to a better Christmas as well as an inspired life.

Tingle, jingle—all the way!

Introduction

Even Santa can't drive two sleighs at the same time!

Yes. It would be nice if Christmas were different this year. Yes. It would be nice to have a celebration that made sense. Yes. It would be nice to celebrate Christmas without too much food, too much to drink, and too many bills. Yes. It would be nice to evolve our celebration to something more sacred and meaningful.

As we prepare to celebrate Christmas, it always takes us to the essential character of Jesus and His teachings, pitted against the unrelenting nature of commercialism. We struggle with contradictions as we try to reconcile these two worlds. One world connects us to the glow of our spiritual essence, while the other connects us to all things glittering. This tug-of-war can cause significant amounts of anxiety and stress. To reconcile these two worlds effectively, it is important that we align our daily lives with the universal principles that Jesus demonstrated to us. This, however, is no small task. All we know for sure from our own birthday experiences is that we enjoy it most when the celebration reflects our true essence. That's what Christmas should do for Jesus; it is, after all, a celebration of His birth.

In order to celebrate anyone we must first know that person's essence. As nontheologians, what do we know about Jesus' values, His teachings, and His way? What was most important to Him? If we were to take a snapshot of Jesus, what would be His soul's desires? What would make His heart sing? What would you do if Jesus asked to wash your feet?

We know that when planning birthday parties, most people have an underlying theme that reflects their interests or likes. They collect tractors, have a passion for golf, or enjoy sailing. Children are very easy. They are usually passionate about something. After a few minutes of thinking about someone, we usually get an idea about that person—if we really listen when they tell us about themselves. Maybe they love dogs, cats, or butterflies. Maybe they love to read, write, or draw.

When we think about Jesus, what comes to mind about His passions and what brought Him joy? Even though His life was very different from ours, what was His underlying theme? What attributes did He display that made Him stand out? What was it about Him that gave such staying power in the hearts of so many people for so many years?

We know that His life was dominated by love. He spoke of love of God, love of others, love of self, and love of our enemies. His main teaching was about our connection to the divine and the importance of forgiveness. He taught us about how to align our hearts and minds with the divine in thanksgiving. He taught us to see the goodness in others as well as ourselves, and to lift up those who are marginalized. He invited us each to follow our own star and to shine our own light by recognizing ourselves as gifted. He challenged us to take a radical shift away from a material world to one of inner harmony. His teachings seem to reach far beyond the realm of emotions or thought; in fact, they seem to encompass an attitude of kindness and connection toward all of life. How do we express this way of life, or integrate it into a celebration, when it seems almost counterintuitive to our everyday world?

What kind of things did Jesus do?

He fed the hungry. He freed the prisoners. He healed the sick and demonstrated the dignity of all people. He was a voice for the voiceless, and He assisted the poor. Welcoming strangers and extending forgiveness was His way of life. Probably the most challenging teaching of Jesus is to love our enemy. Who wants to do that?

What did Jesus not do?

He did not teach about the importance of material possessions. He did not seem to buy big gifts, but He did seem to be known as exceptionally generous. He did not seem to put people down or leave them out. He did not hold grudges or plan revenge. He did not blame others, nor did He avoid pain by pulling rank. He did not remain silent in the face of injustice. Probably the most difficult thing He did not do, was judge others. How is it possible to not judge others?

What did Jesus promote?

He promoted a fair and just society, and living with an open heart. Stepping life up a notch seemed to be his underlying message. Forgiveness was the tool. Love was the answer. He seemed to promote becoming childlike. This did not mean to be irresponsible; it was more of a way to embrace the joy of a child and to live life with the love and awe of a child. He promoted love, peace, and joy, which are all the elements for the underlying universal celebration of Christmas. His teachings promoted a kinder, more sustainable world, one of inclusion and acceptance of all of life. Along with that, He modeled a way of being strongly rooted in and connected to a divine presence. He promoted living life large, being fearless and strong because of a foundation of love. He promoted the sense that our connection to God was possible by going within and connecting with this vast universal force.

To celebrate the essence of Jesus, it becomes clear that we must develop some essential elements of the sacred. It would also seem important to integrate some of the core teachings of Jesus on a daily basis. In order to do this successfully with the offsetting demands of the secular commercial world, it would seem imperative to create a new world order as well as a new spirituality. What would this new spirituality look like? If we were well grounded in the sacred laws would we be as easily influenced by the consumer trends?

When is a celebration a celebration? When is it not?

Through the media, the marketers, and the madness we can feel pressured and vulnerable, especially at Christmas if we have not clearly dealt with the duality within us between the inner sacred world and the outside demands of the secular world. Skilled marketers know our tendencies toward this duality, and they capitalize on these as a way to make money. Since is not possible to ride two reindeer at the same time, or for Santa to drive two sleighs or "have two masters," the only way to avoid the marketing traps is to reconcile the duality within so that there is unity of thoughts, word, and actions.

In order to do this effectively, it is important to get grounded in some sense of a spiritual reality that resonates with our lives—mentally, physically, financially, emotionally, and spiritually. This book suggests ways to reconcile this split between the material and the spiritual worlds so that we can live in a more integrated way. Its main purpose is to invite us to rekindle our magical childlike wonder and connect to our divine essence. By reconciling this split, we let it become a backdrop to living Christmas as a way of life. When we live in this way, we get to know what my good friend means when she says, "It is obvious that the overspending and the overdoing of Christmas have failed, leaving us with a big whole in our bank accounts as well as our hearts."

It seems obvious that it is time to develop a better way to celebrate, to do the things that matter, and to be free to extend this spirit on a daily basis. It is time to contribute something important and become a person who lifts and shifts the world's view to a growing sense of the connection to God, to ourselves, and to others. It is time to embrace our commonalities, understand our differences, and become our best self.

Since Christmas magnifies everything that is going on in our world, this book focuses on incorporating order and spirit into our daily lives. That way, when Christmas comes, we are magnifying things like peace, love, and joy—if we have integrated them successfully in our daily lives. There is nothing more beautiful than spending time with people who project love, promote peace, and radiate joy as a way of life. We want to be with them. We want to soak up their goodness. Somehow we magically feel better about ourselves when we are with them. In their presence we feel valued, seen, and heard. By living from this place of total love peace and joy. It is my belief that it would be possible for us to tune in more to our inner media and less to the outside media, so we too can contribute positive vibes to those around us.

After many years of stress and confusion, I realized I had to find ways to cultivate my own beliefs that were in line with the presence of Christmas instead of the presents of Christmas. Even though I was puzzled by the amount of stress and anxiety experienced by so many people during Christmastime, a season intended to be one of reverence and holiness, I was challenged with the same issues, as I would often lament, "Christmas is just so much work! I am so tired of re-creating the whole thing every year!"

What is your ideal Christmas?

It would seem an ideal Christmas would be based on principles and concepts universal in nature, as well as the underlying elements of peace, love, and joy. It would only make sense that it would include personal preferences as well as integrated spiritual aspects and personal traditions. These principles inclusive in their own spiritual natures would be possible for all people, everywhere in the world. It would seem that under the hum of anxiety, we all have the longing for the basic elements of peace, love, and joy, regardless of our backgrounds. Through the process described in this book, it is possible to have the opportunity to examine the patterns of real love, joy, and peace, so that when Christmas comes, it is a day to celebrate from these principles.

If we embrace the concept that we are all connected, is it necessary to include those who are disruptive, disrespectful, and/or violent in our space?

The basic principles of Christmas have the potential to improve our ability to respond to life events. A countercultural movement away from consumer-focused living and toward a more compassionate way of living might be a big shift, but one that is nonetheless more fulfilling. Behind the Christmas message are the essential elements of the sacred and, perhaps, a blueprint for successful living. If these principles were adopted for use on a daily basis, the celebration of Christmas would flow as naturally as spring into summer.

With the understanding of the beauty of our spirituality, it becomes more apparent that the Christmas Spirit can help us bring light to the world's darkness. If we become the star and spread light to those around us, it might help to create hope for those in despair, or it might help offer clarity in the midst of confusion, or it might just lighten someone's load along the way.

This book explores universal spiritual elements that I adopted in the creation of my ideal Christmas. These elements are based on the principles of Jesus, which are universal in nature and can be implemented by anyone, anywhere, at any time. These elements are about learning to shine with delight and to jingle with brilliance from the inside out. It is a Christmas celebrated in JBO.

A Bit of Christmas History

December 25 was chosen as the date to celebrate the birth of Christ, around AD 320, even though there appeared to be some confusion about the actual date that Jesus was born. Being near the winter solstice, this is a symbolic time of year, as the longest nights of the year are now over, and this is celebrated in different ways in many different cultures.

The celebration of Christmas had its own struggles over the years, as a result of conflicts over religion and politics; because of this, in some years Christmas was celebrated, but sometimes the celebrations were banned. This situation did not stabilize until the 1800s. Christmas Day first became a legal holiday in 1836, in the United States (in the state of Alabama*).

In 1822, Clement Moore wrote the poem "A Visit from St. Nicholas". It was in this poem that Santa was first physically described: "He had a broad face and a little round belly that shook when he laughed, like a bowl full of jelly." The story of Santa Claus is believed to be loosely based on the story of Saint Nicholas, a fourth-century bishop known for gift giving, charity, and generosity. Sadly, Santa Claus eventually became a symbol of commercialism.

Since its beginning, Christmas has kept the same basic meaning of bringing light to darkness, giving and receiving love, and connecting with our true spirit. Throughout the history of Christmas celebrations, there has been an underlying theme of peace and goodwill. Jesus is a great model for these qualities, and we can implement His way in our daily life.

---

* didyouknow.org/Christmas/history

Jesus Factor

"No one can serve two masters. Either you will hate one and love the other, or you will be devoted to one and despise the other. You cannot serve both God and money" (Matthew 6:24).

"I am the light of the world; he who follows me will not walk in darkness, but will have the light of life" (John 8:12).

"Share your bread with the hungry, sheltering the oppressed and the homeless …" (Isaiah 58:6–7).

Part 1
Opening

Jingle Bell Disorder (JBD)

> Probably the reason we all go so haywire at Christmastime, with the endless unrestrained and often silly buying of gifts, is that we don't quite know how to put our love into words.
> —Harlan Miller

It is a Call to Remember

It is a call to remember,
Our true essence,
Our innocence,
Our magnificence.
It is a call to believe,
In something greater than ourselves.
In miracles,
In magic.
It is a call to celebrate,
To lighten up,
To play,
To tingle.
It is a call to sanity,
To freedom,
To simplicity
And more jingle.

As discussed previously, Jingle Bell Disorder (JBD) is a term used to explore ways to bring meaning, harmony, and peace to our lives so that when Christmas arrives, it is possible to truly celebrate from peace, love, and joy. If we were to sum up the essence of JBD, it would be to make sense of the discrepancies between the pulls and seductions of the material world and the eternal requirements of the soul. In so doing it is hoped that we will discover ways to connect with our divine sparkle and live connected to this sparkle.

When I had JBD, I was not comfortable with material things, and I was not comfortable without them. I was not comfortable speaking up, and I was not comfortable being silent. I was not comfortable having everything, and I was not comfortable having very little. I was not comfortable with my own poverty, and I was not comfortable with others' poverty. I was not comfortable at all. I was basically uncomfortable with all aspects of my life.

When someone suffers from JBD, it feels like being split inside. There are many actual causes, including illness, isolation, and fear. When you have JBD, it is as if parts of you remember a better way of being, but the rest of you has forgotten. It is hard to believe that a basically sensible person could be pulled in so many opposing directions. But that is what happens, as anyone who has suffered with JBD can affirm.

You might be saying, "JBD—I know what that is. It is that sinking feeling in my gut I get when I hear the first sounds of Christmas."

Christmas sits in the perfect place for experiencing the divide between the material and spiritual world, and it is also the perfect place to reconcile these differences. Since Christmas challenges us to stretch our hearts, it is the perfect place to create a new reality. It also stretches our pocketbooks and brings our inner and outer contradictions to the forefront for attention. It would almost seem that these contradictions and conflicts are placed before us so that we can discover the mystical element that lies somewhere in the middle.

How do we deal with contradictions? How did we fill that place inside us that feels empty? Do we buy? Do we eat? Do we drink? Do we blame?

What are our biggest contradictions?

JBD has many causes, but one that easily comes to mind is the demanding fast-paced culture we live in. It can wear us down and clutter our minds. The feeling of being cluttered and confused intensifies the sense of being isolated, and this can create a great deal of anxiety.

Technology has given us many gifts, but it also reminds us that we are falling behind. We are plugged in to the demands of the fast-paced world, but we might be unplugged from the person beside us. As we keep track of all that is going on in the world, it can seem be difficult to keep up. Even though we live in a hyperconnected world, we can have the sense that we are separate and disconnected. The sense of being connected to our phones but disconnected from others, as well as from our spirit, can cause a great deal of anxiety. This anxiety can become the base for fueling consumer-oriented promises of the perfect material solution.

Another cause of JBD is our lack of fun. Christmas is best if we can maintain a child's heart and innocence of play. To lose this is to lose a sense of awe and amazement. Play and innocence go hand in hand for a good time, and Christmas can be the perfect playground. As Albert Einstein once said, "He who can no longer pause to wonder and stand rapt in awe is as good as dead; his eyes are closed." If we could remain in awe and wonder, Christmas would be all it is meant to be.

Financial difficulties can cause anyone to break out in a full sweat, but at Christmas it seems to become compounded with expectations and command performances. It can be difficult to stay on on budget when expectations, peer pressure and traditions collide. Christmas memories, and some clever marketing tools swim together in our minds to influence our decisions.

Perceptions, expectations, and attachments are the perfect ingredients for creating a toxic chaos cocktail at any time, but when added to the demands of the Christmas season, they can produce nightmares instead of dreams of sugar plums.

Being attached to certain outcomes, expecting certain things to happen, or perceiving insults when they are not intended all can take the glitter from the intended glow of the celebration. It is as if they form a film over the underlying meaning of the holiday, obscuring our true sight. One of the biggest gifts we can give anyone is to provide some slack for others especially others going through changing, challenging life events.

Change is difficult at any time, but at Christmas it may threaten our attachment to the idea of things going a certain way. Change may threaten our expectations. It creates insecurity as well as upset. However, change is constant, and developing a plan to implement change in our daily lives might be helpful. For example, getting divorced, losing a spouse, encountering health problems, or becoming unemployed are all situations of change to which we have no choice but to adapt. It would be beneficial for us to learn to be able to adjust by dropping attachments, releasing expectations, and allowing our perceptions to be flexible. This is the way to embrace change as it comes on a daily basis.

Can you think of an expectation that you have for Christmas that might be causing you discomfort?

Is there someone or something that you are attached to that is causing you to lose sleep? If you let go of the attachment would you have more peace?

Can you think of a time in your life when you encountered change? If you changed your perception of the change, allowing yourself to be flexible, was the change easier to accept?

Another cause of JBD is the big divide between the rich and the poor. The growing inequality between the haves and the have-nots is very prevalent at Christmas. A living-wage or minimum-wage job might supply the necessary everyday requirements for living, but it will likely leave little for the added expenses that Christmas brings. The unemployed have little to celebrate at Christmas and may feel shame for not being able to provide for their families. They also might feel anger and envy, instead of excitement, as they observe others with great material wealth.

However, I suspect that in the bottom of the soul, especially on Christmas Day, there is a cry, a longing in every heart for a fairer and more just society. The cry may be smothered or silenced with food, alcohol, or material possessions, but whether we are rich or poor, I suggest that this cry is still there in our depths.

What can you do to be a voice for the voiceless?

How can you ask for what you need and require?

In what way can you provide a service to others that enhances both your life and theirs?

There is another cause of JBD that is worth noting: our sense of self-worth. This feeling of worthiness goes hand in hand with our sense of self; it is a sense of our innate goodness and our confidence. A confidence that comes from knowing our own goodness and worth helps us have a true connection on this earth. Lacking this confidence can limit our view of our self and others. To gain a true sense of self is to gain confidence and clarity in our abilities to shine forth goodness. Our goodness has no religion. It has no limits. It is how we were born, but some kicks and bruises along the way can make us forget. To gain a true sense of our goodness is often the strength we need to move forward through multiple fears and limitations to a life with unlimited possibilities.

There are many causes of JBD, and we could explore them forever. However, the biggest reason for JBD remains the lack of connection to the vast world of the eternal current of spirit that runs through us all. Being connected to the force of our divinity that Jesus tells us about, that Jesus leads us to, and that Jesus lives is what will bring order to our lives. Connecting to the universal flow of grace provided by God gives us the strength to live life through different eyes, to hear with different ears, and to act with different responses. Our spirit connection helps us detach from our sad story, our need to be right, and our need to win. It helps us transcend our own needs so that we can be of service to others. It connects us with a force for good, and transports the soul to a more joyful, fulfilled life.

What ways have you found effective to connect to spirit?

Overstuffed, Overcooked, and Overdone

A friend of mine shared with me some of her experiences with JBD. Her childhood history with Christmas was mostly positive. However, when she started her own family, she decided that they were going to always have perfect Christmases. Early in the fall, she would be looking for hints about what her family would love for Christmas so that she could find those things on sale.

She shopped, cooked, cleaned, decorated, and organized family gatherings until she was feeling more and more overwhelmed and tired. As luck would have it, before Christmas her children would change their minds about what they wanted for gifts, which resulted in last-minute shopping. The family would eat all the Christmas baking, so more last-minute cooking was needed. After Christmas Day, she was exhausted and completely dissatisfied, and she realized this was a symptom of JBD.

As the years progressed, it seemed that the more she did to make a perfect Christmas for her family, the more she lacked Christmas spirit, and the less enthusiasm she had for any celebrating. As a result of her trying too hard for perfection, no one in the family was experiencing the peace and joy of the season.

Finally, she came to her senses and was able to see the insanity of it all. It was time for a radical shift in thinking and acting. Once she could see this, she was able to change, moving away from the heavy burden she had placed on herself and her family for Christmas. Now her Christmas has become much lighter and more enjoyable, full of fun, hope, family, and friends—a day to be fully present.

As we think of our own time at Christmas, we might recollect some pressured times in which we did not feel connected to the earth, the sky and to all of life. We might have been over cooked.

We can also think of others with full-blown JBD.

We have seen or been this lady with JBD. Bent at the neck, she somewhat resembles a turtle, with her head hidden in her shoulders, almost coaching her body to protect her from herself. She stands in the line waiting and hoping that her credit card is not already maxed out. She is still breathless and panicked from racing through the aisles, grabbing and clutching at anything to fill the cart.

We recognize her, especially if at one time or other we have been there in the lineups at Christmas, completely disconnected, unconscious, and overdone from the conflicting demands of the season. As she carries the large load of parcels out to the car, she stands totally still, wondering where she left her car or if she even drove one to the store.

We all know the gentleman who hits for the comfort of his own bed on Christmas Day, desperate to escape the knot in his stomach. He pulls the covers over his head, hoping to protect himself from the emotions that he is unprepared to handle. His children seem to know that whatever the blankets provide for him is more important than their need to share this special time with their father. They play quietly, as they do not want to bother their overdone dad.

We all know the man who starts eating when he hears the sounds of Christmas, stuffing himself with a large bag of chips, a pizza, and a full container of ice cream. He stops at fast-food restaurants and devours a week's supply of calories on his way to and from work. He can rationalize that he needs all the extra calories to help him soothe his seasonal anxiety, which smolders just beneath the surface, barely quelled by all the extra fats and carbohydrates.

We all know the guy who buys extra booze when Christmas is coming. He plans to use the extra alcohol to share with all the family and friends he will see over the holiday. But, secretly, he knows that he'll need extra drinks to smooth over whatever rough spots are ahead. If there are no rough spots, he will need a little extra to lighten the so-called fun times. He hardly remembers Christmas with his family and he didn't end up sharing much of what he bought. He was in a slump.

Jesus Factor

"For I know the plans I have for you ... plans for welfare and not for evil, to give you a future and a hope" (Jeremiah 29:11).

The Gift of Memories: Remembering, Celebrating, Believing

> I might look green, but I am no Christmas tree.
> —Phyllis McCarthy

Sift Through the Memories

Sift through it all.
Sift through the memories, sister.
Sift through the memories,
Of Christmases past.
Sift through
All the emotions,
All the memories,
And exchange the unwanted ones
With lighter kinder ones.
Keep the lovely leftovers,
That speak to you
Of your wonder,
Your magnificence
And your bright inner light.

Christmas brings with it memories. In an instant, we can be transported back to a moment in time as if it were today. We can feel our grandmother's embrace and her soft cheeks on ours as we listened to her read "A Visit from St. Nicholas". With one whiff of a turnip puff, we can be four again, watching Dad make the special dish for Mom. The aroma of fresh-baked apple pie can take us back to the table on Christmas Day, when everyone was happy and together. These smells, although seemingly ordinary, can provide us with snapshots of people's faces and how things were on a particular Christmas. It does not take much for the memories to make our emotions bubble up, taking us to places that we might have long forgotten. Some of the emotions are soft, some are uncomfortable, and some are a mixture of both.

The memories of baked cookies, excitement, and laughter may sit close to memories that are not as delightful. Somehow they all take their place inside us, popping up on occasion. Memories can be confusing, as we live with all of them inside us all the time. The constellation of memories running amok through our cells can produce some very strange reactions. Sifting through them is beneficial, as it provides an opportunity to process and let go of the unpleasant ones.

Memories come through us, or to us, from a variety of past experiences. Just the sound of the first Christmas song can start a groundswell of memories of Christmases past. From these memories we can piece together a blueprint for what constitutes a good Christmas. This awareness is not only important for us to know for ourselves, but it also allows us to communicate with others what is important to us. This is especially important if we are to combine our Christmas celebration with those of others who each have their own storehouse of memories.

Memories can be selective. They can gloss over things we wish to forget, and they also make things seem better than they actually were. Memories can also serve as an excuse to blame others and not take responsibility for our free-floating anxiety or our vast array of unmanaged emotions.

Some memories we hold with sadness, resentment, or negative recollection could be a gateway to freedom and love. Letting go of them provides space for new things. Inside each memory is a gift and it is our responsibility to discover these gifts as we sift through the memories of our past Christmastimes.

Finding a way to sift through these positive and negative memories can be helpful. Sifting through the memories is an effective way to discern which memories to keep, which to let go of, and which to transform into something better. Memories are a way to build traditions, so it is important to review the memoires to see if the traditions are still appropriate.

This makes me think of a lady who, at Christmastime, always cut her turkey in two and cooked each half in a separate pan. Her new husband found this strange and puzzling. Her explanation was that she cooked the turkey this way because her mother always did it this way. When her husband asked her mother about this tradition, she explained to him that she cooked her turkey that way because she only had two small pans.

One person may have positive memories associated with having a Christmas tree—finding it, decorating it, and enjoying the lights—while another person may be haunted by unpleasant memories. One person may enjoy the peace and quiet of the season by spending time in solitude, while another person might enjoy a more secular focus, such as festive parties with lots of presents. Our present Christmas experience usually reveals something about past experiences.

When combining Christmas memories, it is easier if the blueprints of both parties are closely matched. If we have similar ways of celebrating, our challenges will be more manageable. It is more of a challenge to successfully integrate highly contrasting blueprints. For those with different cultures, religions, and types of memories, it might be more difficult to merge and combine. Certainly, sifting through the memories and discovering the current values makes it easier to discover a mutually agreeable plan for the season.

What is your favorite Christmas memory?

When I think of memories, I often wonder about the past of a sparkly elderly lady whom I met briefly at the grocery store. She seemed full of joy as she gave in-depth details of the Christmas dinner that she had by herself. Most people would tell this as a sad story, because we have been programmed to think that spending Christmas alone is a bad thing. Instead, she transformed her story into sheer delight. She spoke of her lace tablecloth and fine china. She had everything her heart desired, and every food prepared to her exquisite taste. Her joy was almost contagious. Her conversation went something like this:

> *I love my Christmas meal so much. I have it just the way I like it. It is so delightful to be alone and to have no one drunk,*

no one crying, and no drama. At Christmas there is just me and a perfectly prepared meal. Even thinking about it makes me excited. I did not aspire to be alone, but being alone is so much better than I ever dreamed.

What kind of memories do you think she had? What do you think inspired her to enjoy her meal so much?

Stuck in the Chimney with You

I am stuck in the chimney with you,
And I don't know what to do.
We have too many things in our packs,
And it's breaking our backs.
You have run up the bills,
And I want to run for the hills.
You want to glow and be glad,
While I have just gone bad.
And I am stuck in the chimney with you.

Christmas Challenge

When I think of the challenges that some people have with Christmas, I think of a conversation I had with a gentleman on an airplane. When the subject of Christmas came up, he openly discussed how Christmas could be really crazy when a person chooses to marry someone from a totally different family background. He grew up as an only child, conservative and logical by nature, but he married an enthusiastic, flamboyant, and free-spirited lady from a large family.

She loved Christmas and all the associated excitement and hype, while his idea of Christmas was a quiet day with a nice meal. During the year, he focused on carefully budgeting and investing their money for them to be able to buy a nice home and contribute to educational funds for their children. She spent money easily, buying gifts for everyone in her large extended family, as well as cooking large feasts for multitudes of people.

He told this story with a lot of humor, as he described the many gifts, the funny gifts, the re-gifting, the food, and the people. He related many outrageous episodes that had happened when their two families got together to celebrate Christmas. He laughed almost uncontrollably about having to rent a trailer to haul the gifts home after the holidays.

For example, his father, who was used to quiet, would attend the combined family dinner sporting an egg timer around his neck. After the meal, he would announce that he was setting the timer for thirty minutes, and when it rang, either he was leaving—or the rest of guests were.

In contrast, his father-in-law was deeply religious and found that getting together for a church service was the most important part of the celebration. His father-in-law knew he did not attend church and did not like parting with money. When the collection plate was passed around, all eyes were on him, and he always gave in to adding money to the collection.

He described in detail the space in his house that was required for unused gifts. Each gift was marked with the giver's name on it so that they would be sure not to give it to the person who had given it to them. He spoke about the plastic cuffs he got to keep his sleeves up, similar to the ones men used in earlier times. Another gift was his deceased aunt's salad bowl, which someone had given them, complete with some "aged" dried lettuce in it. The recycled gift drawer had a life of its own. Many gifts stayed there for life, as they were too ridiculous to re-gift, but others came in handy for other gift-giving occasions.

It was clear from his sharing that, even though this was challenging for him, he really enjoyed being a part of this family and blending the different values associated with celebrating Christmas. This family found a way to negotiate and appreciate their created blueprint with good humor and fun.

Sifting Through My Christmas Memories

When I reflect back through my own Christmas memories, I first think back to my mother's memories as part of my heritage. The following were in notes she wrote:

> *Nestled behind a row of Balm-of-Gilead trees stood a large two-and-a-half–story house, which was my first home. It was an eleven-room house with a front porch, very close to the main highway. The highway was not hard surfaced, as we know them today. In those days, they were narrow and rutty, and could get very muddy after the rain. In winter when the snows were deep—and I mean deep—it was impossible at times to keep the roads open. The old North Wind could play havoc while blowing so hard and piling drifts so high.*

She described the excitement of returning home for Christmas after she had been away:

> *I was all excited about getting home for Christmas. I was met at the station with a horse and buggy. I arrived home to a nice warm fire in the kitchen stove. Mother sat by the stove, knitting. She had a freshly baked batch of her white bread cooling on the table. I wasn't long getting a slice of bread and butter.*

The Christmas just before I was born, my mother and my brother (closest in age to me) were away from our family. She needed to be near the hospital because winter storms, road conditions, and the time of my upcoming birth were all unpredictable. My father stayed home with my older siblings. My mother described this too:

It was the first Christmas I was away from home. Even though the day was long, it eventually went by. ... It was Saturday, and my daughter arrived, with loads of black hair and red cheeks.

While thinking back through my own memories, I think of the family farmhouse nestled between the rolling hills. I think of the sweet smell of the freshly cut fir tree sparkling with lights. I think of the boxes of Christmas decorations, many of them homemade. The treetop angel was always packed in its original box, even though it was tattered and taped.

From her perch on the top of the tree, the angel oversaw many Christmastimes. An orange, some ribbon candy, and a gift filled the stockings. Usually this gift was found long before Christmas. The best part of the day was having time to play, as most of the work on the farm was canceled on Christmas Day.

As a child, I was very curious and into everyone else's business. It came as a big surprise, almost a shock, to find out the truth about Santa Claus. How could that be missed? I guess it was only normal to question and query every story after that discovery.

I remember going through the pasture in deep snow with my sled to get our Christmas tree. This was an important assignment, and I took it seriously. It was always challenging to choose the right tree, as it was difficult to decide when the tree was covered with snow, what it would look like covered in lights. It was amazing how the tree would always look so different after it was in the house and decorated.

One year, when I was returning home with the tree, I remember getting my foot stuck in the deep snow. After some time and with great struggle, I managed to free my foot but not my boot. I arrived home without the tree, the sled, or the boot. By the time I got home, my foot was nearly frozen. Lucky for me, I was not in trouble. Instead, I got to put my feet near the wood stove and was given hot chocolate to drink. The tree, the sled, and the boot arrived later. I remember the kindness and attention I received as if it had happened yesterday, and I have often craved that same response when experiencing difficulty.

I also remember the preparations for the school's annual Christmas concert. Not being gifted with a good singing voice, I was often asked to lip sync. One year, because I could not participate in the singing, I was given a solo verse to say at the beginning of the concert.

This poem—"The Presents," by Marchette Chute—is still in my memory:

I told them I didn't want mittens.
And they've given me mittens again!

I especially remember the long drive to church on Christmas Eve. There were usually eight of us in the car. We were covered in blankets and on our best behavior. There was always a very distinctive feeling in the church on Christmas Eve. The candles and flowers made the service extra special.

During the church service, I was generally focused on Santa. On the drive back home, I remember watching out the car window, looking for Santa in the sky. I am quite certain that on one occasion I did see the reindeer flying past the moon. Even though it was late when we arrived home, the traditional fish chowder and homemade bread that we ate was a welcomed closure before bed. This meal always tasted best on Christmas Eve.

The first day of school after Christmas was always uncomfortable. It seemed that the other students got so many gifts, all the latest and greatest gadgets. Whenever I was asked about my gifts, I just made up a list. If the teacher instructed us to write a paragraph on our Christmas holidays, mine was usually embellished to sound much more impressive than it actually had been.

I didn't know how to write about the delights of being together, of the church service, or even of the quiet moments with jingle running through my veins. I didn't know how to describe the thrill of flying down the hill on my sled. I didn't know how to describe watching the tree lights blink, of being in total awe of the beauty of the tree found in the back fields that later looked so elegant in its new location. I didn't know how to write about the sparkly warmth I felt as I smelled turkey cooking.

Language could not describe the silence, the sacred moments between the words. Because I had no words, I made up a story. Generally it included the gifts the other students received as well as the ones I could only dream about.

Looking back, I can see I didn't realize how blessed I was to experience an overwhelming sense of family, of togetherness. I forgot, or took for granted, how the soothing sacred rhythm of the earth joined with the sacred rhythm of the sky, providing a deep sense of peace. The farm provided us with a way to survive regardless of the situation. We knew how to be independent and interdependent. I took for granted that I would always know what it was like to live heaven on earth. I thought it was silly to mention that my heart was so big and as full as my stomach as we knelt and prayed thanksgiving after our scrumptious meal. My story was perfect just the way it was, I just didn't realize it.

My birthday came just after Christmas, which was problematic because it seemed to be overlooked. Gifts were often given at Christmas to cover both occasions. Because of this, I had to become the marketing manager for my own birthday. The main aim of the marketing blitz was to make people realize that my birthday was a separate event from the birthday of Jesus. It worked well for a while.

However, while sifting through the memories, I finally realized just how special my birthday was. Since I was born shortly after Christmas, my mother sacrificed being home for Christmas so that I could be born safely, as I mentioned. We lived quite a long distance from the hospital, and since it was winter, she put my well-being and my life ahead of spending this special time with the rest of the family.

Our memories help us understand the world. From our memories, we form beliefs, associations, and perceptions, and it is from these that we build values. These help us to understand. Our memories show us things not necessarily as they were, but as we remember them. If we sift through them carefully, we just may be able to transform some painful ones so that we do not continue to carry them forward.

Sifting through an old memory can help us to see the gift it contains, as well as to give us a new perspective on a troubling recollection. To move forward, we need to be aware of the impact of memories on our everyday life. As we look back, we realize that what matters most is the time we spent sharing, laughing, appreciating, playing, listening, and having fun.

Do you have a memory from a past Christmas that you would like to let go or transform?

Jesus Factor

"And while they were in Bethlehem, the time came for the child to be delivered. And she gave birth to her first-born son and wrapped him in swaddling clothes, and laid him in a manger, because there was no place for them in the inn" (Luke 2:6–7).

The Gift of Forgiveness: Bringing Forgiveness Home for the Holidays

If we really want to love, we must learn how to forgive.
—Mother Teresa

Forgiveness is choosing to love. It is
the first skill of self-giving love.
—Mahatma Gandhi

The best gift we can give to others and to ourselves is the gift of forgiveness. Forgiveness opens us up to love, which is one of the fundamental elements of Christmas. Forgiveness is the most useful gift for loving relationships and for a good life. Jesus spoke of forgiveness a great deal, so it would seem appropriate to implement forgiveness as a gift to the holiday heart.

Early in life, it seems that our hearts know how to love properly. We seem to know how to instantly let go and get on with life when we are hurt. Someone takes our toy, and we cry. We shake ourselves off and find another wonder of the day. We seem to be born with an innate sense of forgiving. It is as if every child is a natural champion when it comes to getting over hurts and disappointments.

Life changes all of that. Our journey through life is never perfect, and we encounter incidents that are unfair, unkind, and unnecessary. All sorts of things can happen. We get hurt; we hurt others. Forgiveness then becomes paramount, because if we leave these painful matters unresolved, our hearts become congested, and then instead of be filled with love, there may be such things as fear, anger, guilt, and grief dwelling within us.

If you do not have a forgiving heart, you might as well stay home. It is forgiveness that brings you back to you, which is the universal love within all of us.

> *If you harm someone else, it is like a pothole in your road of life. You need to find a way to make amends so that you can make your road all smooth again. Generally all you need to do is to apologize. The words "I am sorry" are very powerful. If they forgive you, it is their choice but the main act of asking will help heal and restore you.*
>
> *If someone harms you, go directly to God and ask for help with forgiveness. God will help you with it.*
>
> —Hazel Munn

Forgiveness provides an opportunity to clean up the debris from the hurts and betrayals we sustain. It also helps us to reconnect to the flow of love in our hearts. Each and every process of forgiving will take its own length of time. It somehow resembles the process of grief, winding in and out of our bodies; and then one day, by the grace of God, we realize the process is complete. The incident, the importance of the relationship, and even our willingness to forgive can affect the length of time that it takes.

Forgiveness came to my rescue when I became good at holding grudges. It is a mystery how it works, but with constant daily connection to divine assistance, it is possible to forgive, to let go, and to move on. I learned the hard way that only I suffer if I do not forgive.

When we broaden our perspective of life, we process forgiveness differently. For instance, we learn to take time, to look at different perceptions and our own contribution to the situation. As we grow and mature, we learn to stop blaming, naming, and gaming. It is only with maturity that we realize the importance of forgiveness, regardless of what happened. Forgiveness is deciding to let it go, deciding to learn from the situation, regardless of how painful it might be, or how insensitive or hurtful the actions of the other person might be—or how we might perceive the situation, actions, or person to be. It is summoning up the courage to move forward to freedom, secure in the knowledge that we are worth the effort.

Life is too short.

Time is too precious,
To hold a grudge,
Or keep resentment.
Set yourself free.
Set others free.
You will never regret,
Letting go—forgiving—moving on!
It is the best gig in town.

> I get busy forgiving as soon as possible. I move the heaviness
> out of my heart as soon as I can. I choose forgiveness first.
> I might not continue the relationship as before but I forgive
> everything as soon as I can. I know it is the best way to love me.
> —Anne Comeau

Revenge doesn't work. Retaliation doesn't work. Holding on does not work. The only thing that works is forgiveness. Until we forgive, we will continue to justify our reactions to injustices. We will blame others and focus our energy on the outside of us. Forgiveness comes when we take responsibility for our own welfare. There is a sweetness that arrives in our heart after forgiveness is complete. This sweetness makes the process very valuable. It is not just a wise choice, it is the only choice.

Because the path to forgiveness is not a predictable one, it can sometimes appear to others, or even to ourselves, that we are not trying hard enough. However, what we may be failing to realize is that when we are not able to forgive fully, it is sometimes just because the wound has not healed enough, or because that particular injury might just take longer to heal. Forgiveness takes its own time. It is a mystery, as well as a gift that comes after the process has been completed. As it is with surgery, so it is with forgiveness: it seems that even though the resentment or anger have been removed, there is still some healing required which often needs divine assistance for the process to be complete.

The prayer Jesus taught us says, "Forgive us our trespasses as we forgive those that trespass against us," and this reminds us of our own requirement to both give and receive forgiveness. We all need forgiveness. Forgiveness is a bit like a dance; we forgive others, and then we need forgiveness ourselves. It is sometimes difficult to forgive others, but it also can be difficult to ask for forgiveness. We've all been on both sides, so we know how hard it is. Equally difficult is the process of forgiving ourselves. When we mess up, it can be a challenging choice to forgive. Sometimes it is easier to run the story over and over in our heads, instead of forgiving and moving on with a lighter heart.

How do we make amends to someone we have hurt?

What is meant by the phrase "Your apology is a good start!"?

What did we contribute to this situation? How can we change our behavior so we do not repeat the same thing? Is there an action we can carry out that shows genuine remorse?

Forgiveness Is the Fuel That Runs Santa's Sleigh

I have found it helpful to implement a forgiveness plan as a part of life. This plan changes and evolves with time. What I have found most effective is an evening routine that includes a review of my day.

As part of my daily plan, I end my day with routine structure. It begins with gratitude. I list the many things I was grateful for during that day. Next, I list in writing any areas that I want to let go of or need to forgive. I take note of areas where I feel the need to apologize and make amends. Sometimes I become aware that I need to connect with a person for some emotional honesty, to clarify my perception, or maybe to work toward reconciliation. If I have a situation that is problematic, I ask for divine assistance as I write about it. I have found it helpful to use different-colored markers as I write in different directions on the page.

My list-writing process looks something like this:

I would like to forgive _____
I feel _____
I need _____
I felt like this before when _____
I understand you may not be aware of _____
I ask God to help me to let go of _____
I want to feel _____
I know you would not purposely hurt me, so _____
I would like to change _____
I request _____
I am glad _____
If I took a broader perception of this it would be like this _____
I took care of my personal health today by _____
As I am in the process of forgiving, I pray for the health and well-being of _____

    This process is finished when I have nothing else to write. Generally it looks like a finished piece of art. The colors all mesh together, and as I keep writing all over the page, it is often completely filled with color and design.

    This process also provides a framework to apologize for my own wrongdoings. By working from this awareness, I have found it possible to keep more relationships intact and to restore injured relationships faster. Forgiveness is not easy, but it is powerful.

Monkey on the Turkey Platter

Another technique I have discovered that is effective about forgiveness is what I call the "Monkey on the Turkey Platter." When something happens and I feel myself contracting, I decide whether or not I want to pick up this particular monkey and include it on the turkey platter. In other words, I picture Christmas dinner (the turkey platter) and decide if whatever it is (the monkey) is something I want to have around for the holidays.

    If I pick it up and churn it over and over, it fills my cells with negativity. In my mind I travel down a life span of twenty years and look back to see if it had been worthwhile to add that monkey to the platter. Often, as I refocus myself back in the present time, I realize I am delighted that I had not picked it up. I then decide to let the incident go.

It is a tremendous feeling to create a totally different reality and to not be offended, not be upset, not be hurt or wounded. It is very freeing to realize that if you do not take it on, there is nothing to forgive. This is a very powerful gift to give oneself.

Kiss and Make Up under the Mistletoe

Forgiveness is not about forgetting the incident or pretending that everything is okay. It is a process of understanding, reflection, and personal growth. Often, when we forgive in haste, in order to let go or to keep a relationship intact, the forgiveness may be premature. If the issue is not resolved and the required changes are not made, the process may require more time.

At Christmas, one may be in haste to forgive so as to restore the holiday and the festivities. The danger lies in the fact that the forgiveness may have been granted while the resentment is still smoldering. Sometimes it is wise to allow the festivities to continue and agree to revisit the situation at a later time.

Preventative Forgiveness

When it comes to forgiveness, it is essential to review perceptions. Our perception is only our way of looking at things. We develop perceptions from our beliefs, experiences, and backgrounds. We can experience the exact same thing as a friend, and yet, during a discussion about it, find out that we had a totally different take on the situation.

This is why reviewing our perceptions is a very important element of forgiveness. Is there another way to look at this situation? If you were an outside party would you look at this situation differently?

If the situation does not resolve, play Truth, Lies, and Perceptions. This is a simple game that involves the second party.

First, ask that person to play. Provide the rules of the game. They are really simple. You give the situation, and then you say, "I thought _____." Next, ask the person if what you thought was the truth, a lie, or a perception. The perception usually has a lie and a truth to it. For example, I was visiting a friend and she was not engaging in any conversation for a long period of time. I thought she did not want me there, so I left feeling quite rejected. When I played the game I found out my thinking was wrong. My friend had a headache, and although she was not engaging in conversation, she wanted me to just be there.

What does this have to do with forgiveness? It is actually *preventative forgiveness*. As you check your perceptions, you often find there is nothing to forgive.

Christmas provides us with the perfect platform for forgiveness. It is one of the primary components of Christ's teachings, as well as a season that has many twists and turns that may require forgiveness. If we make forgiveness an important part of everyday living, it is easier to approach the season with an open heart. An open heart makes each of us very irresistible under the mistletoe.

Is there a something that changing your perceptions can help you to forgive? Is there a lesson to learn?

Who Is the Real Village Idiot?

When the soft snowflakes stopped falling, the sun came out and melted the snow on the walkways. Sylvia, a retired teacher, was on her way to her former school for a double celebration: the annual Christmas concert, plus the school's fiftieth anniversary. As she made her way to the door, she pulled her scarf extra tight and tugged at her mittens. Sylvia had remembered to wear the special silver hairpin that she always wore to past Christmas concerts. This morning, she had applied an extra layer of makeup to hide the lines of time.

As she entered the school, she could see all the Christmas lights blinking and the decorations welcoming everyone to the celebrations.

The out-of-town license plates she had seen on the cars in the parking lot had been confirmation of the attendance of some highfalutin politicians. Even from a distance, she could see some of the dignitaries huddled together with her former bosses. She still remembered the stress of past supervisions and took a deep breath to remind herself that those days were over. The best part of retirement was that she was now on equal footing with her bosses. Today she had no title and no responsibility—and nothing to prove.

She felt anxious entering the school, and glanced around in search of a familiar face so she could anchor herself. She always felt a need to connect with someone to ease her initial discomfort at public gatherings. Chatting with someone about the weather and a mixture of ordinary things always helped her with this transition. The gymnasium was alive with the scent of pine needles and the aroma of coffee, and the smells brought her attention back to the past. Today it spoke of memories, celebrations, and celebrities, but nothing could hide the faint underlying odor of sweaty sneakers.

As she observed the beautifully decorated stage and the corner Christmas tree, she couldn't help but think of how versatile the gym was. This gym was easily transformed into today's celebration, a school formal, an assembly, or a Friday night basketball game. She had spent so many years in this gym, and yet she was once again amazed at how the students always knew how to make it fit every situation.

In the distance, her eyes caught sight of a former student, Marvin. As he made his way across the room, she could see that he exhibited the same openness, sweetness, and confidence she remembered. Marvin had spent two years in her classroom, where he had repeated sixth grade.

Today she saw a man with immaculate grooming, his clothes tailored to fit perfectly, with a demeanor resembling that of a statesman. People seeing him for the first time today would probably assume he was a top-level official. They would never guess that for years he was known as the "village idiot."

Sylvia thought it must have taken a great deal of courage for him to come back to this school where he had experienced little success.

Not only did he have academic difficulty, but his limp and lisp isolated him from his peers. With some inner guilt, she thought that this school should have done a much better job to support him and protect him from all the harassment he went through.

Still from a distance, she noticed him approach an important government official and sit down beside him. As she thought back to many of the favored students from the school, she wondered if any of them would be able to muster up enough courage to do that. She watched his cheerful demeanor and was curious about his life; how he had been able to take years of put-downs and still develop such a positive outlook. She knew she lacked the courage to apologize to him for not doing her part to make his school life better, but today she would carve out a chance to talk to him.

She could tell that he knew something that she did not. The student who had been made fun of the most seemed to be the happiest person in the crowd. Over the years, Sylvia had seen many students bullied or made fun of; most of them suffered lifelong repercussions. But she could see that Marvin was not like this. He seemed to flourish in spite of it all, and she wanted to know his secret.

Picking up a crust-less egg sandwich made with soft white bread, Sylvia eased her way in his direction.

"How are you, Marvin?" she said, accidentally, on purpose, starting the conversation.

"Great, ma'am!" he responded, just as he always had.

"What are you up to these days?" she inquired, feeling a bit silly for sounding so boring.

"I am keeping people on the road." He provided this well-rehearsed answer with a smile.

"I heard you are a great mechanic. A friend of mine told me that you did her a huge favor when she was having financial difficulty. She mentioned you fixed her car and then filled it up with gas at no charge."

"People say lots of things," Marvin responded. "I just try to help people out. I have a soft spot for women who have a batch of kids and good-for-nots husbands."

"Marvin, I am wondering if you can help me."

"Help you out if I can." He looked puzzled as to why a former teacher would need his help.

"I am not quite sure how to say it, as my question is about you. When you were a student, I remember you being treated rather poorly, and sometimes the other students were really mean to you. How do you stay so positive and good-humored?" Her question was bold and would have stirred anger in most people.

"Well," he said, and then he paused before he continued. "My mother always knew I would be dumped on because of my limp and my lisp, and because I found learning hard. She taught me that people who are mean are just poorly brought up and unhappy. Because of this, they look for people to dump on. She would tell me, 'Never call bad-mannered people out, as they will hurt you. Really confuse them, and don't listen to them. Pretend they are telling you something kind or nice.

"She gave me a shiny stone to keep in my pocket and, whenever someone was mean to me, I just rubbed my special stone to remember what she told me. Because of my stone, I always knew that I had a choice to feel bad, or not. I could be mad at what mean people said, or I could not listen to them. When I did not listen to them, I did not feel bad. Instead of feeling bad, she taught me to do something kind for myself or someone else."

As Marvin took the stone out of his pocket to show Sylvia, he continued to talk about his mother. "My mother had two favorite sayings: 'Never take the mask off the Lone Ranger' and 'Don't roller skate in a buffalo herd.' When she talked to me about mean people, she asked me to picture a special bus in my heart, and she said that all the people on my bus were kind and had good manners. They were funny and good-natured. Since it was my heart, I got to be in charge of who got on my bus.

"As I look back now, I can see that she was teaching me not to waste time on mean people. I only spent time on the people on my bus. I think she was just trying to help me out."

"Your mother was remarkable," Sylvia stated. She thought about the wisdom of Marvin's mother and how she helped him make the best of such a difficult situation. At the same time, she felt a knowing sting that she had missed the opportunity to be on his special bus. She wished she could have the opportunity to do it all over again.

"Yeah, my mom was remarkable," Marvin agreed. "She was always happy. I guess because she was very good at understanding folks. She knew when I went to school that you folks might be too busy to help me out, so I had to do it myself. At night she would help me with what happened at school that day. My mother and I almost always found a way to handle things. Guess she loved me enough to teach me about people, especially the mean ones, because they have a reason for doing what they do."

"I saw you give your seat to one of the big shots today. That was kind of you, considering he can be so gruff and mean."

"I would do that for anyone. He has bad manners and a mean streak because he did not learn a better way. He never made it on my bus, but I always felt sorry for him. He just seemed to be mean for no reason. Maybe he needed a mother who would have loved him enough, someone who could love his mean streak out of him. Hard to tell what bad things happened to him. Whatever it was that happened to him, it made him a grouchy old man," stated Marvin.

"Now that you are older, what do you do if someone is mean to you?" Sylvia asked, eager to learn his secret at last.

"I just give them to Mamma. She was the forgiveness queen. She has been dead a long time, so I figure she is in a better position to handle them. I say, 'Mamma, this one is for you. Handle them, will you? I have no time,'" replied Marvin.

"What usually happens after that?" Sylvia asked.

"The people either leave me alone, or they get real nice, real fast. Gotta go now. Nice talkin' to you, ma'am. Merry Christmas," Marvin said.

"Merry Christmas to you too," Sylvia said as she watched him leave the room.

He was leaving before the concert, and she decided to do the same. She didn't feel like staying any longer.

After she got home, Sylvia undid the silver hairpin, letting her hair fall softly over her shoulders. It had been a truly interesting day. Only now, she was the student seeped in her own transformation.

Did she have enough time left to make her life remarkable, as Marvin had done? Who was she going to let on her bus? Forgiveness! Who needed her forgiveness? Who did she need to forgive? Her vision of life had changed in such a short span of time.

As she sat down with a cup of tea and the newspaper, she couldn't help but wonder, Who is the real village idiot?

She knew who it wasn't.

Jesus Factor

"And forgive us our debts, as we also have forgiven our debtors …" (Matthew 6:12).

The Gift of the Present

*It is good to be children sometimes and never better than
at Christmas when the mighty founder was a child himself.*
—Charles Dickens

All we really have is now—this very moment. However, it seems so much easier to be someplace else. Living in the present moment requires a focused intention to keep ourselves from being distracted. It seems more natural to swing back and forth between the stresses of the past and the worries about the unknown future. It can almost feel like a child swinging on a swing, back and forth, but seldom stopping in the middle which is the moment that is now.

Not being in the moment takes us away from what is readily available to us in the present. When we are preoccupied, we miss this marvelous moment that is directly in front of us. By missing this instant, we are missing our connection to the presence in everything, such as the smile of a child, the beauty of a sunset, or the plea from a friend who needs our help. We can miss the beauty woven into our lives.

This moment, now, connects us to what is going on in our lives. It is an automatic way to disconnect from the constant chatter in the mind. Breathing is an instrument that helps us focus on this one moment. Conscious breathing can slow us down and help us focus on what is important, as breathing mindfully is a link to the present. Being in the moment connects us to our calm center, our oneness with the divine.

All the important things that we are searching for in life cannot be found from worrying, regretting, or obsessing as these take us away from the present. Important matters can only be found in the moment, as it is the present that provides us with the opportunity to connect with the joy that flows through us. It also provides us with the opportunity to choose something different. If we are fully present and aware of the moment, we can decide if we want to change it to a greater possibility. It is the moment that provides the magic ingredient for life.

Experience the Moment

Stop what you are doing, and look around you. Be aware of where you are and what surrounds you. Take a mental snapshot of this moment in time. Be with yourself, fully aware of all that you see, smell, hear, and feel, to help you absorb the moment. Become aware of your breath and how it flows in and out of your body. Notice the landscape around you, the colors, the sounds, and the movements. Listen to the background sounds. Be silent, and in this moment of stillness, feel an expansion of all your senses of all that is. Breathe. Listen. Be aware.

If it Hadn't Happened

If it hadn't happened
I would not have noticed
Your infinite beauty
As you stood so close beside me.
If it hadn't happened,
I would not have noticed
The full clear moon
Perfect, to direct Santa's sleigh.
For it was what happened
That took me to this moment
Full of magic and delight;
It took me to you.

Christmas as Being Present

The Christmas season is a very challenging time to practice living in the present. It is not easy to stay in the moment, with all the stress of preparing for the celebrations. This time can lend itself to triggers of past memories and worries about the future.

All the obligations at this time, all the lists of things to do, all the command performances, all the duties, and all the pandemonium, can become overwhelming. Instead of being fully engaged with the joy around us, it is easy to become distracted and let the moment slip away.

However, it is at Christmastime that being present is truly vital; joy, love, and peace are the fundamental reasons for the season. These can only be found in the present moment. When it is possible to connect to joy, love, and peace, and to live from this connection, then you are living the real presence of the season.

It is one of the ironies in life that the more we stay focused on the present moment, the more we can let go of the demands we place on ourselves. The present moment helps us to slow down and experience all that life is offering to us. There are plenty of opportunities to be in the moment, such as enjoying the simple act of wrapping a gift, trimming the tree, or just sitting in silence and watching the lights sparkle. When we are able to stay in the present moment, we can be present to ourselves and present to others, which is the greatest gift of all. When we are present to someone and with them at that moment in time, we communicate to them that they are valued and divine.

Santa Might Have an Edge

The present moment has a strong transformational power for people experiencing JBD. People with JBD tend to feel uncomfortable with the moment, often because they are uncomfortable with their emotions. As emotions surface, it may be easier to become distracted and to ignore our feelings by moving into the past or the future. It may seem easier to become busy just to avoid these feelings, but, eventually, it becomes vital to be with them. For instance, when you have a broken heart and you do everything but feel the devastation, the cries of the heart eventually do squeal out, loud enough to gain attention. When we attend to emotions in the moment and are present to them, we are better able to free ourselves from the grip of unmanaged emotions.

Too much emotional pain is uncomfortable, and our initial response might be to avoid it. Sometimes it takes more effort to avoid the pain than to face it. Once we have exhausted ourselves with distractions from our own emotions, it becomes easier to be present with them. Being present with them seems to lessen their power. As they lessen in intensity, we can often discover the gifts hidden behind the emotions, and letting go becomes easier. By letting go of the strong hold of emotions, and by being fully present to them, they either lessen or disappear, allowing us to regain our wonder and connection to life. It is not necessarily that the pain will disappear completely, but by being fully present to it, we make it possible for the pain to diminish, and, eventually take its place in the rear view mirror.

Fox and Owl

"What time is it?" asked the fox.
"Now," said the owl.
"Now?" inquired the fox. "What time is that?
"It is the only time there is," replied the owl.

Best Christmas Gift

Dealing with emotions can be the best Christmas gift we give to others as well as to ourselves. When we think of dealing with emotions, we can compare it somewhat to cleaning our glasses. When we clean the lenses, we can see more clearly. When we are transforming difficult emotions, we are cleaning our internal vision to improve clarity. When we clear away the guilt, anger, or regret, we are better able to see the beauty in the moment.

By gaining this clarity, we can attend to the moment presented. We do not transfer the emotions to someone else or project the underlying residues of our emotions onto others. We are more capable of letting our bright spirit shine. We can cherish the ones around us, and add a touch of wonder and sparkle to everything. With clarity, we are in a better position to respond with love rather than to react. We are more aware of our needs, and we have the space to express ourselves honestly.

The process of transforming our emotions can lead us to the moment and all that it contains. With greater clarity, we can look at changing some distracting "-ings," such as judging, reacting, controlling, and interfering, which are out-of-the-moment actions. By being present, we can become aware of other "-ings," such as loving, accepting, responding, and caring.

The Moment and the Mountain

Downhill skiing demands being totally in the moment. When the skis meet the sacred silence of the mountain, they insist on total attention in order to arrive at the bottom safely. Any time the mind drifts to the past or to the future, the skis demand that the mind redirect attention back to the moment. Even mounting the ski lift takes full attention in order to make the successful transition.

The poles, mitts, and goggles take their places, as we, ever so present, sit on the lift. Each move is crucial to the moment's success. From our vantage point on the lift, there is so much to take in: the snowdrops on the trees shining in the sun, the young skier who has made his winding down the mountain an art, or perhaps the warmth of the sun on our chilled cheeks.

Staying in the moment, however, allows us to connect to the heartbeat of the mountain. There is a rhythm and motion to winding down the hill that transcends time and space. The crunch of the snow as the edge of the ski cuts into it requires full attention, and joining the magic of the rhythm provides the backdrop to experience the very moment where heaven meets earth.

There are no moments to miss on the mountain, even though some are not as critical as others. The breathtaking view at the top of the mountain is always so different each time. Sometimes the snow crystals provide their own light show. These moments are more relaxed than other more perilous moments, but they are still significant because of their soothing effects on our soul. This constant array of natural delights connects us to a presence far greater than ourselves.

It would be unfair not to mention the importance of the moment after-ski ritual. There is a snapping sound to the tired boots as they leave the skis and stand with the others. Not accustomed to walking, the boots clamor on the wooden floor of the lodge, in search of a snack and a warm drink.

There is an array of smells as the warm air hits the cold face with an unofficial welcome back from the mountain. The awaiting egg-salad sandwich and hot tea provides little time to dismantle hats, coats, and mitts. Each bite is delicious as it touches the taste buds. Having this special ceremonial snack requires attentive appreciation of each bite, providing a perfect ending to a tremendous day.

Awe of the Moment

Another way to connect to the present moment is through stillness and silence. Being still and silent helps us to become more aware of what is going on in the moment and what is available to us in that moment. In stillness, there is neither conflict nor a point of view. It is especially enjoyable before sleep.

When silence and stillness are part of sleep hygiene, the body stays quieter all night and awakens feeling rested. Christmas is the perfect time to be still, and it is also the perfect time to be mindful of all the blessings that are available to us. If we can really listen to the children singing at a Christmas concert, if we can really be with a gift as it is unwrapped or pay close attention to the person who gives us a gift, the season brightens with magic.

However, it can be difficult, if not nearly impossible, to stay with the moment, especially at Christmas, because of the cascade of things to accomplish. Sometimes it seems like it would be easier to join the reindeer flying through the air, but when all is said and done, the magic of Christmas lies in the moment and being present to it.

A "Now" Way of Being

The people we most admire are often those living mostly in the present moment. We feel special around them because they are fully present to us, through attentive listening and by being supportive and respectful. There is no reason for judgment, just an accepting attitude of trust and warmth. They engage with us in a clear, calm, and respectful way.

It is enjoyable to be with these people because we feel heard and cared about. Present-moment people are attractive because they are close to their own spirit. There is nothing more exciting than going on an adventure with someone who is fully present, as such people laugh easily and often.

Stop, look, and listen. Sometime in your busy day, stop and take note of what is around you. Watch the beagle next door sniff his way around the yard; listen to the birds singing in the tree; watch the children walking in the rain, with their bright-orange and purple boots. Be with yourself, fully aware of all that you are and how special you really are. Breathe, and just be with your spirit.

The way we breathe is a powerful metaphor for how we are living. For example, if we are breathing shallowly, we may be living that way too, fear based and anxiety focused. When we breathe deeply, using deep belly breaths, it allows us to be more oxygenated, which in turn helps us each to be more present in our life. How we breathe and how we live affects how we act. When we become aware of our breathing, we become more aware of our actions. When we become more aware of our actions, we will be more mindful in the present.

The Now Watch

Now is the perfect time,
To breathe, to just be;
To be grateful:
For all the joy
That is present right now.

It Isn't Even Tuesday Yet

Monday, just before Christmas, while grocery shopping, I met a beautiful lady who had an enchanting ability to be totally present. She was a friendly gal who provided a very uplifting experience during the few brief encounters we shared. She was so present in a conversation that even just a brief encounter lifted and shifted ones spirit.

This day, she had a distinct glow as she shared a snapshot of her life and her plans for Christmas. She was shining with delight and eager to spend time with her family. We laughed and chatted as we exchanged celebration plans, and then we each went on our way. The rest of my shopping seemed more enjoyable as a result of this uplifting encounter.

Three days later, I was shocked when informed that this enchanting lady had been killed in a car accident. It was a difficult concept to comprehend, since her spirit was so brilliant and alive in my mind. In the short space of time since I'd last seen her, someone had lost a wife, a mother, and a daughter, and a community had lost her beautiful presence. All of this happened in such a short time, and it wasn't even Tuesday yet. It hadn't even been a full week since our chance meeting.

Sometimes it takes a shock like this to realize just how absolutely imperative it is to be present to each moment, to everyone and everything. Moments are vital. The moment is all we have.

The Present from the Goose or the Gander

On a bright sunny April afternoon I was walking on a busy city street. My mind slipped into what I call "building a fairy tale tomorrow." In my mind, I was trying to create a heart that would symbolize a heart for humanity, a true Christmas heart that would include all people, without judgment. I was trying to figure out what a heart would look like that contained unconditional love, unconditional joy, and unconditional peace.

I knew that it would have to be a heart that made sense, with a quality of beauty and an element that served humanity in some way. My mind was totally consumed with this concept until I was abruptly brought back to the moment by a severe bite on the back of my leg. My immediate thought was that it must be dog, but when I looked down I saw feathers, not fur.

Once I escaped the biter's grasp, I realized it was a big Canadian goose. Puzzled by such an experience, I moved quickly to a safe distance from where I could observe this goose. What I saw was that this goose was sitting with a companion under a railing beside the sidewalk, with what appeared to be the indiscriminate sole purpose of biting anyone who walked past.

My first reaction to the pain of this bite was anger, but I soon realized that any confrontation would be of little value, as yelling at these two geese would be a waste of time. Nor did it seem sensible to report the incident to the Goose Union or the CEO of Goose Management! After calming my heart from this scare, I felt I was left with little recourse but to let the anger go. Instead of feeling angry, I decided to be grateful that I had no apparent open wounds.

Just before resuming my walk, I glanced to the right and caught a glimpse of an unusual arrangement of rocks. As I looked more carefully, I saw that the rocks formed a huge heart, which was filled with water and surrounded by beautiful shrubs and trees. I then realized that the goose had inadvertently brought me back to the present moment, enabling me to view a heart of all the goodness of humanity that I had been building in my imagination.

State of Being Present

Once we see the importance of present-moment living, it is possible to increase this way of being in our daily lives. When we become more present as a way of life, we also become mindful of all the wonder and awe in our lives. We notice the birds singing to us, the flowers on our path, and the smile of the elderly man we pass on the street. This way of being reminds us of all the miracles and magic that is right in front of us throughout our daily lives. Being present and mindful lifts our spirits and connects us to all that is available to us in every moment.

Being present keeps our lives in plain view, connects us to our spirit, and leads us to a realization of our connection to all.

As I followed a robin on its path to a nearby tree, I noticed that many other robins were already in the tree. What a beautiful sight! There were about twenty red breasts turned outward. It looked like the still barren tree was full of red blossoms.

As we adopt this way of being, it appears easier to accept what is actually going on, without being hammered by the past or worried about the future. It provides a freedom of sorts, with the capability of connecting us with the awe of life. It also provides the perfect opportunity to choose again and to build a different future. Answers come to life questions once the chatter stops, and we each get to be an observer of life in the moment. Living in the moment allows the reality of that time to earn its due attention. Infused with the moment is a deep connection to a presence of gratitude, and this is the key to freedom.

10 Ways to Be Present

1. Watch a baby sleeping.
2. Observe a Christmas candle flickering on the mantel.
3. Turn off your cell phone so you can really tune into your breath.
4. Listen to the crunch of snow beneath your feet.
5. Watch a shooting star.
6. Be fully present in nature.
7. Taste each bite of Christmas dinner.
8. Watch a child come downstairs on Christmas morning.
9. Pay close attention while wrapping a present.
10. Give your full attention to the person talking to you.

What distractions are you using to avoid feeling your feelings?
Are you fully present to others?
What part of your story are you using to stay in the past?
What fears are keeping you focused on the future?

Jesus Meets the Women at the "Well" Mart

A distraught elderly lady sits beside her empty shopping cart on a bench outside the mall grocery store, sobbing into her tissue. She is relatively unnoticed by the other grocery shoppers as they hurry to pick up food for supper. Many Christmas shoppers are totally unaware of her, focused as they are on getting the necessary items on their lists.

A small child sees the lady and wonders what is wrong. It wasn't so long ago that this little guy cried like that when he fell on the pavement and scraped his knee. Before he has a chance to tell his mother about the sad lady, she hurried him off down the aisle.

Just before the lady finishes using her last tissue, Jesus appears and sits down beside her.

"What is wrong?" asks Jesus. "I would like to help you."

She does not recognize Him but is very happy to hear a kind voice.

"I am so discouraged," responds the lady. "I can't find anything to buy for Christmas dinner. I am used to buying a turkey and the usual Christmas fixings. But this year is different, as all my children are coming home with their spouses and children. Everyone is eating something different. It seems like there is nothing I can buy, with all their different diets, eating plans, and food allergies. As I look at my list, I cannot figure out one thing to buy," she finishes, relieved that someone cared enough to listen to her.

"Let me see your list," Jesus says. "Maybe I can help."

She passes Him the list.

Grocery List for Christmas Dinner
No meat
No dairy
Only certified organic
Only certified sustainable
No sugar, no artificial sugars
Only locally grown products
No gluten

No Trans Fat, no saturated fat, no hydrogenated oils
Absolutely no cholesterol
No carbs!

"That is quite a list!" says Jesus. "I understand why you are having trouble finding anything to buy. I can see your dilemma. Do you mind if I make a suggestion?" He asks.

"I would love any suggestion, as I have no clue what to do," replies the woman.

"Why don't you just be with your family, enjoy their company. Make some foods that you will enjoy, and ask them to do the same. You can let them know that their different needs are too difficult for you to accommodate. Then you can enjoy every moment with them, and spend time playing with your grandchildren."

"That's a great suggestion!" she says. "I could try that. I could make some of my favorite recipes and have them on hand for everyone. My favorite is turnip puff, so I will make that—at least I will be happy. I will get some games to play with my grandchildren. That is what I like best anyway."

"Be more Mary than Martha," Jesus adds.

"Great idea!" she says as she smiles and walks toward the grocery store.

Jesus Factor

"Martha, Martha, you are getting worried and upset about too many things. Only one thing is important. Mary has chosen the right thing, and it will never be taken from her" (Luke 10:41).

The Gift of Gratitude:
It Is a Line to the Divine

> Do not spoil what you have by desiring what you
> have not; remember that what you now have was
> once among the things you only hoped for.
> —Epicurus

There is no better place to live than in a state of gratitude. Every day there are many opportunities for profound appreciation and gratitude. As we look around with eyes leaning toward gratitude, it is possible to see more of the great things life has to offer. Even when things in our lives are not what we want them to be, or even if we are facing a huge challenge, we can find many things for which to be grateful. It seems a bit of a paradox that when it is the most difficult to be grateful it is also the most important. Gratitude is like the tipping point toward seeing what is right in our lives rather than what is wrong.

Make Room in the Inn for Gratitude

Gratitude appears to follow the concept that what we focus on expands. When we focus on being grateful for the good things, the more good things we will experience in our lives. The power to focus on the positive, on all the wonders that life offers, creates an environment for things to increase. It seems that gratitude is even more necessary when things are not going smoothly. Gratitude provides the necessary focus to see the gift, the growth, the strength, and the support that are available.

At Christmastime, because of the extra stresses and pressures, people with JBD find it difficult to focus on being grateful. However, in order for us to fully enjoy the season, gratitude needs to be fully entrenched in our lives, an integral part of our way of being, so that when the season comes, appreciation and gratitude are part of the main menu.

Marathon of Gratitude

When I think of a gratitude story, the first that comes to mind is an experience of a friend who is marathon runner. She had trained well and was feeling confident in her ability on race day.

Halfway through the race, she started to become nauseated and considered dropping out of the race. She remembered how a former coach had taught her how to switch her focus when things got difficult. At first, she switched her focus to the beauty around her, such as the river flowing over the rocks, the beauty along the running trail, and the strength and courage of the other runners.

Her focus on this surrounding beauty helped her feel supported by life itself, and gradually she started to feel better. Next, she focused her attention on gratitude. She thanked her body, and each part of it, for helping her to accomplish something that was very important to her.

After she finished paying tribute to each body part, she realized all her body parts were working well, except her stomach. Finally, she thanked her stomach for letting her know it was time to slow down and notice all the beauty along the way.

As she crossed the finish line, she was very grateful: she had achieved her goal, even though it had been a struggle. She was also very grateful that her coach had taught her the simple act of shifting her focus. In so doing, she got to experience all the beauty along the way.

Gratitude as a Line to the Divine

Since everything in its truest sense is from the divine, showing gratitude provides a direct line to the divine. Gratitude awakens us to the sweetness and wonder of life. As an intentional way to live, gratitude shows us what is going well.

It is more than a thank-you, it is a more of a spiritual recognition and a connection to a greater reality. It changes our lives and makes us more appreciative of the good we have. Gratitude focuses us on what we have, and keeps us from looking at what we do not have.

Gratitude is a Line

Graitude is a line
To the divine.
A simple word of thanks,
Puts a tickle in our tanks.
It is the icing on the cake
On anything you want to bake.
Gratitude
Sharpens our attitude.
It is what makes us feel fine,
As it is the line to the divine.

Gratitude—it is great way to express our appreciation to the divine for all our blessings.

Growing in Gratitude

Living in gratitude can be compared to the life of a flower. Planting the seeds of gratitude resembles the same process as planting flower seeds. When the seeds of appreciation and acknowledgment are sprinkled with love, these seeds grow into beautiful flowers filled with gratitude blossoms. The more seeds of gratitude we plant, the more blossoms we produce, until we have a whole garden of appreciation in our heart.

Flowers blossom more fully when we actively engage in planting seeds of gratitude. This is part of what Jesus meant when He said, "Whatever a man sows, that he will also reap" (Galatians 6:7).

Gratitude Makes the Best Stuffing

From the moment we open our eyes in the morning until we close them at night, we can choose to focus on gratitude. Once we experience the true feeling of gratitude, we want more of it. Being grateful is a self-loving choice. This choice can expand our awareness of all the great things in our lives.

What do you want more of in your life? What seeds and recognition of gratitude do you want to grow? Can you be grateful for some things in your life that you do not like? Do you know anyone whose life would be better if he or she experienced gratitude daily?

Gratitude in our lives is so powerful because it helps us focus on what is going well. With gratitude, we can even learn to look for the gifts we receive from difficult circumstances. It also provides us with the ongoing opportunity to thank our creator for the gift of our life, and for all the wonders, blessings, lessons, and miracles that surround us daily.

When you receive a gift you do not like, you can still be grateful that the person thought of you.

Gratitude Greases the Wheel

Being in the state of gratitude offers an opportunity to experience more fun, more adventure, and to see more of the mysteries and magic in life. When we live in a state of gratitude, we can live more fully and more gracefully. Everybody loves a grateful heart.

Without an appreciation for what is going well for us, many of the great things in our lives can go unnoticed. People with JBD can focus on the negative aspects of their lives, and then they can miss the positive wonderful things. Focusing on the negative can lead us on a journey down the slippery slope of nongratitude, complaining, blaming, and focusing on what is wrong. If we understand that what we focus on expands, few of us would consciously choose to have more difficulty in our lives. The Christmas season provides multiple opportunities for appreciation, and it can be a pivotal time to shift to gratitude.

Slowing Down

Slowing down,
Makes it easier
To notice
All the sweetness,
All the goodness in life.
Slowing down
Provides an opportunity to give thanks,
For food, for clothes,
For all the people, that makes life better,
Easier, kinder, nicer.
Slowing down
Provides a chance to be grateful
For all there is,
For what is important.

A grateful heart just makes life more pleasant.

Effects of Ingrates

It is a challenge to be around people who see the world in an ungrateful manner. It seems to drain the life right out of you. Have you ever cheerfully offered your energy and resources to help someone, and afterward see no gratitude, not even a "thank you," and maybe even a bad attitude instead? Can you think of a time when your generosity has been greeted with a grumble or a grunt? Sometimes a response like this can feel like rejection. Nongratitude can even seem cruel. Although we do not give something merely to receive appreciation, there is great power and importance in the two words thank you.

As an experiment, I opened and held the door for anyone entering my apartment building. It was interesting how much richer my experience was when the person showed some sense of appreciation. In contrast, when someone offered only a complaint about the weather or some other triviality, I could feel my energy slump. In the end I realized the small act of appreciation was like a breath of fresh air.

Gratitude "Seals the Deal" Between the Giver and the Receiver

From knowing how significant gratitude is toward having a happier life, we can be thankful that our parents insisted that we say our thanks. It is why we teach our children to say thank you, even though they may not necessarily feel grateful in their hearts. But we are planting the seed so that someday the gratitude will be in their hearts as well.

These lessons provide us with a powerful way to acknowledge and delight in the good, as well as God, in our lives. Wallace D. Wattles says, "You cannot exercise much power without gratitude, because it is gratitude that keeps you connected with power."

Between the giver and the receiver, gratitude makes this process complete and ongoing. The act of appreciation provides an opportunity for the donor to continue giving, and for the recipient to join the dance of receiving. Gratitude acknowledges the giver and provides the opportunity for increased giving. The giving and receiving dance continues best when the deal is sealed with gratitude.

Shifting to Gratitude

With only our habit
Of a coffee and a bagel,
I sat on our park bench,
Chilled with the morning frost,
And your absence.
At first, all I could see was the thick mist of the morning,
Which resembled
The cover over my heart.
Then, off in the distance, there was a break of sunlight
Sitting in the trees,
Bright and cheery in the morning mist.
It reminded me to shift my focus,

From loss
To soft whispers of the heart,
To love,
To Christmas,
To Gratitude,
For the chance to have known
All the warmth and the dreams
The cold bench had to offer,
When shared with a friend.

Big Red

I am so grateful to my friends who took valuable time and energy to help me find a very special car. Her name is Big Red. From the very first day, Big Red became a reliable friend, and her energy and eagerness supported me on my journey through adversities, transitions, and transformations.

Big Red came to me at a time in my life when I needed special support, and she was my constant companion for fourteen years. She was eager to be of service and provided a steady supply of whatever drives were required. She was ready to go on the coldest day of winter and on the hottest day of summer.

She kept her inner power and could go faster than a speeding bullet when I most needed her. What was important to me was always important to her. Over our fourteen-year relationship, her support and assistance were unconditional and nonjudgmental. She never ran interference on the company I kept or the places I went.

When I was preoccupied or worried about something, Big Red appeared to have the ability to navigate on her own. Sometimes she would just go where I needed to go instead of where I was headed. She had a reputation of sometimes taking wild turns when she had to get my attention to change directions. She was friendly, likable, and reliable. Because of this, and her innocent sparkle, she could sometimes talk her way out of trouble if she got caught going too fast.

Because she was enlightened, Big Red was able to take her share of bumps and bruises, without the need for revenge or resentment. If someone put a dent in her, she just dusted herself off and breezed on down the road. She seemed to find it more worthwhile to use these infractions as learning opportunities.

Because life had taught her the importance of forgiveness, she would choose to resolve issues instead of creating them. She had no problem "fitting in" in the parking lot, and felt neither inferior nor superior to any other vehicles, whether they were bigger, shinier, or had more gas in their tanks. She liked herself enough not to have to change in order to fit in. She was well defined and always seemed to know her beauty.

Big Red had a Good Samaritan quality about her. She always had a box in her trunk to collect things to be dropped off at the food bank or homeless shelter. She started with just a few items, but as time went on, somehow her trunk was usually full, with the overflow in her back seat. She had sharp eyes for spotting anyone who needed mittens from her supply on a cold day.

Big Red provided safety for all her passengers. She kept a careful watch for big trucks and oversized cars that might show signs of danger. Her watchful eye helped prevent any major collisions. Romantic by nature, she loved summer picnics, music, and tender care. She provided shelter if storms interfered with plans. She was flexible and confident, and could transform herself into a truck, a cool date environment, a sports storage shed, or a play center.

Big Red was with me through very challenging times. For me, she is a symbol of loyalty, reliability, and integrity. I am so grateful to have had her as a constant companion for so many years. Together we learned that showing gratitude is essential for a happy life. I am very grateful to Big Red, and I hope she is proud of all she accomplished in life. Big Red aged graciously through this process, and she now proudly lives in a retirement home that understands the value of her life.

Big Red demonstrated that gratitude like; friendship is limitless in its form and expression.

Jesus Factor

"Have no anxiety about anything, but in everything by prayer and supplication with thanksgiving let your requests be made known to God" (Philippians 4:10).

Give thanks in all circumstances; for this is the will of God in Christ Jesus for you.(1 Thessalonians 5:18)

The Gift of Giving: Giving, Receiving, Asking

A Gift Is a Message

The Magi delivered the first three Christmas gifts to the Nativity with a message to honor, to revere, and to celebrate this extraordinary event. Each of these three gifts had a significant message: gold signified a cross cultural value of special importance; frankincense a calming, restorative incense that recognized Jesus' holiness; myrrh was an anointing oil with a healing component.

The first gifts continue to serve as a model for gift giving at Christmas, even today. These gifts were both practical and symbolic, and they recognized the significance of the birth. Like these gifts, any true gift represents an act of love and delivers a message of love. Like the first Christmas gifts, a true gift honors the receiver as well as the giver.

A gift is an act of love and a token way to express love and appreciation for having that person in our life. Its purpose is to bring joy. A true gift is purchased with tender attention to the relationship of the giver and receiver.

The best gift is usually simplistic in nature, with no strings attached. Thoughtfulness, sincerity, and effort in choosing the gift add value to that gift. Love speaks through the gift. Like the first gifts, a true gift honors, reveres, and values the receiver.

Giving and receiving are part of life's greatest joys; they warm our hearts and make us feel important, valued, and loved.

Christmastime, however, brings a whole set of expectations about giving and receiving. There is a great deal of pressure to buy gifts that will please everyone on our list, which can rob the giver of the ability to give from spontaneity and genuine thoughtfulness.

Trying to get the gift just right can add a great deal of pressure. It is easy to see how we get caught in the trap of giving and receiving the perfect gifts under the Christmas tree. All too frequently we get caught up in the idea that the perfect gifts will make us feel better.

Is it possible to have giving as a way of life, instead of just giving the so-called perfect gift on Christmas Day?

If we are really present with people in our lives, and if we really listen to them, it is easier to get them each the perfect gift.

I can think of two gifts that stood out in my lifetime. When I was young, my sister gave me a transistor radio. I took it with me wherever I went. I remember sleeping with it, taking it on adventures, learning the words and tunes to all the songs, and singing along with them. I particularly remember singing along to Bobby Vee's "Rubber Ball." Much later, I received a tennis racket in my favorite color. This made me feel valued and loved. These kinds of gifts reflect the importance of being listened to, cared about, and understood. They brought me such joy.

Can you think of a favorite gift? What was it that made it special?

A true gift brings joy to the giver as well as the receiver.

People with JBD have difficulty with the idea of giving and receiving. Because they may not be congruent with their own spirit, gifts from them may not make sense. They sometimes buy when they are upset or exhausted, so they may be unconscious of the needs or desires of the receiver. They may substitute bigger for better, which removes the feeling of joy and meaning for both the giver and the receiver. Equally important, the receiver with JBD may have difficulty accepting any gift, even though the gifts received might be appropriate and selected with care. It is as if they feel unworthy and so have difficulty receiving.

What are your unique gifts?

What gifts do you give freely and without strings attached?

Santa's Intent Was Good

Even though Santa's intent was good, that does not mean everyone else's intent is the same. Some people may even use this special gift-giving time for their own purposes, even to the extent of hurting another person. Because of this, the gifts we receive can be classified in different categories. When we become aware that some giver's intentions are not always pure, we need to rely on your ability to be perceptive and discerning, a gift we give to our own spirit.

Those gifts which are given without any understanding of or regard for the receiver speak more clearly about the giver. The gift is given to make a point that the recipient is not good enough as he or she is. An example of this could be giving makeup to a lady who never wears any, or giving a weight-loss program to someone overweight. These gifts in and of themselves can just be insulting.

Sometimes the giver feels a need to cover up something about himself or herself, or to gain something from the receiver. The lack of authentic tenderness causes discomfort between the giver and the receiver. An example could be a husband or wife who has had an affair, and then produces a gift of a family holiday instead of confronting his or her past actions with a new sincere and restorative action.

Some gifts are cleverly chosen to strike at the heart of the receiver. The intent is to induce guilt in the receiver. The gift may be great in and of itself, and it may even be envied by others who are not aware of the underlying intent. For example, when a parent buys a gift to play one child against another, with the intent to punish or control the one who may not be complying with command performances. The parent may give a bigger gift, such as larger sum of money, to the child who conforms, and a much lesser amount to the child who has not conformed as well. This may be done in front of other adults and with their approval.

A gift is 90 percent intention. What is the best thing to do if the gift has a poor intention?

The Gift of Time Doesn't Cost a Dime

Your magical and mystical spirit side is the best part of you, and sharing it is the best gift you can give. You give this gift wherever you shine your light of wonder on all you encounter. You know the people who just light up a room when they show up. The same is true for you. It is not always necessary to buy gifts when you are the gift. Your gifts of loyalty, integrity, and honesty shine through any darkness, and they are cherished long after purchased gifts are gone. When you tingle and jingle with life and all its wonder, you provide an amazing gift to others in your presence.

I Know You Do Not Have the Money

I know you do not have the money
To buy me a present, honey.
So let's get together over the holidays
And celebrate in other ways.
Maybe we could take a nice long walk
And have a heart-to-heart talk.
A gift would only get in the way
Of what we really want to say.
The gift of time
Does not cost a dime.
So let's get real and make a deal
And start giving invisible gifts of the heart.

What are the unique gifts that you bring to the table?

The Drama Trap

Although it is generally important to be a good receiver, it is equally important to be discerning in this area. There are as many reasons for giving as there are for receiving. Not all of them are authentic, and it is very important to know the difference between authentic gifts and those with strings attached.

Underlying each gift is a message that speaks to the relationship between the giver and the receiver. It may speak of just one of the parties or both. Although it is important to become a good receiver, it is equally important to be aware that all gifts are not well intentioned. If the gift speaks of manipulation, or a scam that is meant to harm, what is the best thing to do? Do you know how to refuse a gift as graciously as you receive one?

When the intent behind the gift is not acceptable, is it okay to refuse it? For example, I had received a gift that I found hurtful, but I felt awkward about refusing or accepting it. I said my usual thank you, and received it. It never felt right, and it left a bad taste in my mouth. When Christmas came around again and I had a hint I was going to receive the same gift, I expressed my concerns openly and honestly and requested a change. I made it very clear I was not accepting a gift of this sort again. The beauty of doing this is that my emotional honesty appeared to nullify the hurt by the gift, and this in turn improved the relationship.

Gifts with manipulative intent are very different from ridiculous or unthoughtful gifts. An unthoughtful gift can be a mistake or an oversight from a cluttered, overtaxed mind. For example, giving dog food to someone who has a cat, or who doesn't even have any animals, is underwhelming but not hurtful. Since it does not have a hurtful intent, it is possible to graciously accept such a gift and then find someone who can use it.

When receiving a gift makes you feel beholden to the giver, what can you do to make it a win-win situation?

For people struggling with JBD, the gift-exchange experience can be very difficult. They may acquire too much debt and may become too open to the seductions in the consumer world, especially at this time of year. It is difficult to give authentically from an overburdened heart, a cluttered mind, and an empty wallet. In this state, it is very difficult to relax, think clearly, or be truly present.

In addition, such life transitions as health problems, loss of a job, the death of a loved one, and/or divorce can add a lot of stress to our resources, in many ways. Learning to celebrate, even during such transitions, is an art that we can master if we take the necessary time to connect to our spirit daily.

The Importance of Becoming a Good Receiver

Receiving well is a special gift to the giver. It is saying to the giver, "I appreciate you, and I am grateful that you thought of me." Receiving demonstrates that we are not only grateful to the giver but also that we are worthy to receive. Receiving and giving are like a dance. Accepting and receiving gratefully set in motion the openness for more receiving.

Giving graciously sets the rhythm for the dance. Receiving gratefully provides an opportunity for the dance to continue. Sometimes, with a lot of emphasis on giving, the importance of receiving well can be overlooked. The giver leads the dance, and the receiver determines the flow of the dance. In life, each of us has needs, and each of us has abundance. When we put our extra resources into the basket of life, and we receive what we need from the abundance of others in the same basket, we keep the dance in motion.

I have a friend who shared his understanding of the dance of giving and receiving with me. One day when we were out driving, I stopped to put gas in my car. Just as I started to fill my tank, my friend informed me that he wanted to pay for my gas. In my discomfort with receiving, I immediately stopped the gas pump. I thought I was being kind by saving him money. But what I thought of as kindness actually upset him.

He let me know that because I did not fill my tank, I was cutting him off from his giving, and thus cutting him off from his quality of life. He pointed out to me that his quality of life depended on his ability to keep the flow of giving and receiving in motion. He had been in the hospital, in the vulnerable position of receiving. He wanted a chance to give. This helped me to understand that my reluctance to receive was beneficial neither to others nor to myself. It takes both giving and receiving to partake in the dance.

A Gift Like No Other, from My Brother

Having supper at my brother's house is such a treat. He has a cozy place where everything is handy. When I visit, I get to eat fresh fish, tasty veggies, and homemade bread. He often hides dessert so that I don't eat it first. But just as important as the meal are the laughs we have, the type you can only have with those whom you've known for a long time.

While at my brother's, there is always a sense the well-prepared meal symbolizes life at its best. To me, there is a sense of the recipes from our shared childhood—the sacred attention to detail, combined with the well-remembered flavors, contains a gift with a deeper meaning. The meal is a gift of celebration. To date, this gift symbolizes a greater gift from long ago.

This gift dates back to when my brother and I were attending a one-room school with approximately a dozen students. He must have been in fourth or fifth grade. I think I was in second grade, because I had a math book, and nothing good like that happened in first grade. We walked to school together, a journey of about two miles from our farmhouse. It might actually have been shorter, because everything is exaggerated when you are a kid. It seemed like we would walk forever, through and past farms, woodlands, and ugly dogs.

Finally, we would get to the school, which sat on a hill. Behind the school was an unnamed body of water. It wasn't a river, a lake, or a pond like other bodies of water in the area. All we knew about it was that it was bottomless, with stories of missing people and objects. It was rumored that if we fell in, we would end up in China.

Because of the possibility of danger, students were never allowed behind the school. Our teacher, emphasized this rule more than any other—even more than her many prohibitions on fighting, lying, missing homework, or chewing gum. It was clear that if we were ever caught going behind the school, we would be in big trouble. Although we were never told explicitly what would happen, she probably meant that we would get the strap. No one ever wanted that.

I cannot remember who finally decided to explore behind the

school. Probably it had to do with knowing it was forbidden and noticing that the teacher was distracted. As a kid, it's hard to know when joint consciousness tips the scale on decisions, and everyone runs with the pack. Whatever the reason, this one winter day we went on an unauthorized exploration. I remember it was just as magical and exciting to be breaking the rules as it was to be crunching through the snow and sliding on the ice. It was a winter paradise for a kid.

As if it was yesterday, I can remember the crack in the ice, and then without notice, I was hanging on to a piece of ice left jagged from my fall. I don't remember being scared, but I do remember my wool mittens gripping the ice, and my body surrounded by frigid water. I remember looking at my brother for help like a younger sister always does. The other kids seemed tentative to come close to me, but I remember my brother saying, "No we can't leave her here—she has to be home for supper."

I do not recall if it was a joint effort but I do remember, he fished me out of the water with a big stick. Once I got to my feet, we ran back to the school. The bell rang, and we went into the classroom.

I don't remember if we all promised not to say anything, or if it was just an unspoken agreement. I remember sitting in my wet pants and ice-watered boots at my desk, with my math book. I didn't dare take my boots off because the pool of water would have revealed our secret. I also didn't dare ask any questions in case I might be asked to go to the teacher's desk. So I stayed quiet for the afternoon.

I was so happy when school was out and we were on our way home. I felt so free to get away with my wet pants and boots, with everyone out from the threat of the wicked strap. It wasn't until I tried to walk that I found it difficult to move. My mittens were awkward and unhelpful, and my pants, still wet, stiffened in the cold.

The walk home was silent.

I knew my parents would be really upset with me if they learned what had happened. I knew a way to sneak into the house from the woodshed. I managed to get upstairs, change my clothes, and put them to dry on the stovepipe. As I entered the kitchen, I was relieved that my change of clothes went unnoticed. The farm probably provided more important things to focus on than what I had worn to school. Chores and supper bought enough time for my clothes to dry, with my family never knowing what happened.

Now that I am an adult and it is no longer possible to "get in trouble" in this manner, I can acknowledge the courage it took for my brother to rescue me from the water. His steady hand and focused intent should have been given top honors at the time, but they weren't, because we were all too scared to own up to our shenanigans. Looking back, it was so silly to keep this a secret. Our parents probably would have been happier that I was safe than upset about what we had done. His bravery not only made it possible for me to be home that night for supper, but also for me to be at his house for supper so many years later.

The gift of life is a gift like no other, from my brother.

A Gift That Lasts a Lifetime

There was no smell of fresh-baked cookies or plum pudding coming from her kitchen. There was no "bowl full of jelly" or twinkling fairy-tale choirs singing "O Come, All Ye Faithful." There was just the faint stinky smell of the same old Christmas story at Sally's house, completely opposite to the way it had been originally intended. This smell activated past memories of insanity and fear. Her whole body was reacting. Her loudly thumping heart kept pace with her throbbing stomach. She knew she needed a rest; she needed time alone, and she needed time to think. She had lived too long witnessing and experiencing unnecessary heart retching cruelty.

Sally went straight to her bedroom, closed the door, and stretched out on her well-befriended comforter. As she lay on her bed, she started to focus on her breathing and her usual calming routines. When her body started to relax, she noticed a fly on the wall in front of her. It was a relief to watch it and to be distracted by its smooth movements. Without even knowing it, the fly separated her from the pain of the situation. This fly reminded her of herself, as it too seemed out of place near Christmastime.

While resting on her bed, she started to sense the power of change running through her veins. Even though there was no cozy fire in the fireplace, she could sense warmth rising up from her stomach. She wondered if Santa felt like this before starting his one-night journey around the world.

Her thoughts then went to Jesus, and she wondered what He would want on His birthday. Did He want people to be doormats to someone else's behavior, or did He want people who were being mistreated to speak up? Would He like for us to be bystanders when other people were being put down, or would He want us to stand up for them? What kind of gift would He want on this celebration of His birth?

She then remembered how important it had been to her when people stood up for her. She thought back to her high school days, when a very strange man stalked her. He would follow her when she went to babysit, to attend sporting events, and to go out with her friends. She remembered always being so terrified, and in her attempts to try to lose him, she would frantically hide in backyards and churches, and even run through streets. She was even too scared to tell her parents.

This all changed one Saturday evening, when she was walking with a friend, on the way home from a school dance. The stalker appeared. Her friend noticed the frightened look on her face as well as the changes in her behavior. When her friend asked what was wrong, she admitted for the first time that she was being stalked. Her friend then invited her to her house and assured her that her father would be able to help. Her father had been proactive with her family, telling them that when situations like this happened, they were to bring it to his attention. It was with great relief that Sally appeared in their living room to tell her friend's father the story of the man in the blue sedan.

Her friend's father put down his newspaper and his pipe, and he listened carefully. After hearing Sally's story, he got the license-plate number of the blue car that was parked just down the street, waiting for Sally. With this story and this number, he disappeared into a darkened room with huge doors.

On his return to the living room, he assured her that the police already had the man in the blue car in custody; he would be leaving town the next morning, never to return to the area. Her friend's father made arrangements for Sally to be safely driven home. He then returned to his previous position with his pipe and paper.

Looking back, Sally can only guess that this seasoned, well-connected gentleman must have intervened on my behalf and spoken on her behalf about the stalker. Making the man in the blue car disappear from the area for life was probably not as effortless as it appeared to Sally at the time. However, the fact that her friend's father combined his knowledge, ability, and kindness to gift a frightened teenager with safety on an ordinary Saturday night, stood out to her, not only was it an incredible gift in the moment, but also as a prodigious gift that would last a lifetime. This kind of gift changes lives. We all are in a position like this, at one time or other, to pay it forward. Even though it was not wrapped, and it was not Christmastime, could this be a gift that Jesus might give a high five to, as a way of recognizing Him and His birth?

It dawned on her that it was her turn to pay it forward. It was time. Sally picked up the phone.

An Unwrapped Gift

Except for the Christmas tree in the corner, there was no trace of any festivities in the barren waiting area of the local hospital emergency room. This was Barb's third trip here today. She was still so worried about her lethargic asthmatic child, who on good days was fully charged and taking on life full throttle. But today, he was very still and quiet, which was an extreme deviation from his normal behavior.

Barb had always been adept at handling many different situations, and she was accustomed to having her contributions well respected. Her enthusiastic manner and abilities served her well and made her a valuable member of any team.

That all changed when she needed to advocate for her child's medical care. Even though she could feel that her child's life was at stake, she had been dismissed twice already today. The fear of being brushed off again caused her to feel vulnerable at the very time that she needed all her strengths.

Bolting down a big chocolate bar from the vending machine did little to relieve her worries. Her biggest worry was that the doctor would not take her concerns seriously, that he would casually dismiss her again as being an overprotective mother who had little else to do on Christmas Eve.

Sensing her desperation, another more experienced mother in the waiting area asked if she could help. After she realized that Barb's child's life was in danger, she gave her some tools to help. She advised that to have the best chance to be heard as a mother, was to choose language carefully --by using such words as intensity and duration, and taking the emotional tone out of your voice were the most helpful. She already understood the idea that emergency-room doctors were very busy and responded best to facts.

After what seemed like a very long wait, the emergency-room doctor appeared. He listened to Barb's fact-filled story and to her son's lungs, which he found to be clear. He advised Barb to take the child home and celebrate Christmas. In a calm manner, Barb requested a consult with a pediatric asthma specialist.

After some consideration, this referral was made, even though it was not the procedure of this medical system to refer to a specialist when the emergency-room doctor had found no medical problem.

The specialist arrived, listened to the child's lungs, and immediately realized that no air was moving. In a loud voice, he called out to the hospital staff, "We have about three minutes to save this child's life!"

With that, they flew out of the room with the child.

Barb was left behind, alone in the room, childless and quite breathless herself, with the blood-pressure cuff as her only companion. She waited and worried and prayed. Would her son live? She was relieved to know that he was now in very capable hands. But had they waited too long?

When the specialist did return, Barb did not know how to prepare herself for whatever news was coming. "It looks like your child is going to be all right, as he is starting to stabilize. I think we had someone on our side tonight. I will monitor him closely all night."

"Thank you!" she said, almost apologizing, because she knew these words were not enough.

"I need to ask you a favor," the doctor said, stammering on the next words. "I promised my family that I would have breakfast with them tomorrow. Would you mind if I left for fifteen minutes to be with them in the morning? I would not feel comfortable leaving your child without your permission."

Grateful, Barb quietly said, "Sure."

From the fright of the day, to this first ray of hope, combined with all the worry and fatigue, it was almost too much. As the doctor turned to walk away, Barb could feel her body start to react. First she felt her body tremble, as if it was shaking off the night, her knees shook, and her feet were bouncing off the floor, and then, gradually, she could feel the warmth in her chest.

For the first time in her life, Barb knew what it meant to be touched by grace. Her prayers had been answered. On his way, the doctor turned around briefly, and they exchanged a knowing look that it was grace they had just experienced.

"Thank you," she said again, shooting him a smile and a wave.

It seemed like thank you were the only words that she could utter to convey her feelings for this precious gift of her child's life. She continued her prayer of gratitude, extending her thanks onward to the heavens, thankful that her prayer had been heard and answered.

This gift though unwrapped was the best gift of all.

Asking

Dear Santa,

Now that I am all grown up, I am looking for ways to make sense of Christmas. I am exhausted from all the giving and not getting, and I feel like a jack-o'-lantern, with a big smile on my face but empty inside. I hate stupid gifts. I liked the ones you gave me when I was a kid. Can you help me out?

Thanks, Santa!

Susan

Dear Susan,

Merry Christmas! Great to hear from you! I always loved giving gifts to you when you were a child. You were so excited and grateful. You truly believed I would bring you what want you wanted, and I did. Your childlike heart is still inside you. Stop trying to do it all. Lighten up!

There is a simple childlike trick you have forgotten: Ask for what you want. Believe it is on its way. Feel the excitement of it being with you, and then be ready for it.

I want you to be happy. When you are happy, your light shines so strongly that it lights up the whole sky. Your light always helped the reindeer and I as we went on our way. We have missed that.

HO! HO! HO!
Santa

Jesus Factor

"Every good gift and every perfect gift is from above, and cometh down from the Father of lights, with whom is no variableness, neither shadow of turning" (James 1:17).

"Ask and it will be given to you; seek and you will find; knock, and the door will be opened to you" (Mathew 7:7).

"It is more blessed to give than to receive" (Acts 20:35).

Part 2
Maggie's Search for Christmas

Love Is a Toodle-Dee-Doo!

The crumpled reindeer wrapping paper and silver bows lay on the floor as Maggie swallowed her annual Christmas anxiety. *I hate Christmas!* she thought as her tears screeched out to meet the already built-up tension within her body. *Why can't we cancel it?* she would always say to her friends.

This stress usually started in November, in anticipation of the upcoming season that she dreaded most. By the middle of December, her symptoms always worsened, increasing in intensity straight through to Christmas Day. She always ended up at the doctor's office, diagnosed with the flu. The doctor would try to reassure her that she was like many others with a seasonal flu and there was really nothing he could do to help.

This year was different; the doctor mentioned the flu, but followed that diagnosis by asking her about her Christmas.

"What does that have to do with the flu?" she asked sharply.

The doctor did not seem bothered by her tone. He gently mentioned that he noticed in her file that she'd had the flu every Christmas for the last seven years.

"Is there something about Christmas that you find difficult?" he queried.

Maggie was not in any mood to listen to such foolishness. She left the office promptly, saying that she had to get to a meeting. She either required an antibiotic or not. She took exception to the doctor's silly questioning.

On her drive home, though, she did start to reflect on her Christmas. What if the doctor was on to something? He had always been very good with her in the past. He had been so supportive of her during her teen years. It was his letter that had helped her get a college scholarship.

He had even been very supportive of her difficulties with her mother. So now why was he questioning something as simple as the flu and associating it with Christmas? As she became calmer, she started to think that maybe he sensed her inability to cope with Christmas.

What is it about Christmas? she thought.

Christmas was always the same story at her house. She did not have enough money for the presents she wanted to buy, but somehow, she would buy them anyway. Over the years she had watched her mother, who had even less money and was chronically broke. She dreaded watching her mother's antics. Every year, she would tell her mother that what she really wanted from her was a Christmas card with a beautiful and meaningful message. She thought she was being very clear that she did not want any presents. But each year, her mother would tell her that it was Christmas, and it wouldn't seem like Christmas unless she bought her presents.

On Christmas Eve, before heading for the mall, Maggie's mother would fortify herself with some rum as she complained about the weather, the prices, and the crowds. As her mother went out the door, Maggie would remind her that she did not want a present, but if she really must buy her something to make sure it was not a scented product. She knew what her mother would look like when she came back from the mall, and she dreaded the sight that she remembered from previous Christmas Eves. Her mother's smile from the effects of the alcohol would be worn off, her mood would be bitter cold to match the weather outside, and she would be bent over from the weight of all the presents she had bought.

This year, it was difficult for Maggie to feel any warmth for her mother as she returned from her annual shopping spree. She was almost nauseated by the combination of the flu and witnessing her mother standing there looking completely blown apart. Her hair was straggly, and she had two-inch roots in need of a touch-up. Her winter boots were worn to threads. She looked so unraveled and unattractive. Her wrinkled, tired face revealed a sour mood. On top of the heap of presents on the floor, Maggie could see a turtle-shaped wading pool.

"What is that for?" Maggie asked, at the same time scared to hear the answer.

"I thought it would be great for Billy, Sue's little boy," responded her mother, referring to the next-door neighbors.

"Why did you buy something for him?" continued Maggie.

"I'm not sure. It was on sale, and I thought he would like it," her mother answered.

"Yeah, but it's the middle of winter," Maggie reminded her mother.

"Oh, I forgot! Oh well, he can play with it in the summer," replied her mother.

She took all the parcels upstairs, disappearing for the rest of the night to wrap them.

❄ ❄ ❄ ❄ ❄

Maggie knew her mother had been up all night wrapping and putting beautiful ribbons and bows on each gift. When Christmas morning arrived, Maggie's mother handed her a gift. As always, it was wrapped with beautiful ribbons and bows. Maggie was hopeful that she would have a nice gift, but her hope was short-lived. Inside, there was a bottle of perfume. This might have made a nice gift for someone else, but not for her.

Other Christmases, she had been able to compose herself and fake gratitude. However, this year was different. She had not been feeling well and was tired from her college exams. Her history of many Christmas disappointments had finally caught up with her. Instead of her usual thank you, she burst into tears.

"What's wrong?" her mother asked, shocked at Maggie's outburst and lack of appreciation.

"I hate perfume! It makes me really sick! This stuff is horrible! Don't you ever listen?" sobbed Maggie. "I hate Christmas too! It is always like this!"

"How could you hate Christmas?" gasped her mother. "All you had to say was 'thank you'! If I had any idea how ungrateful you are, I wouldn't have bought you anything. I do all of this for you and go to all this bother just because I love you, and what thanks do I get?"

Maggie bit her tongue and continued to sob. She wanted to say that this didn't feel like love. She wanted to say that she hated the fact that her mother spent money she didn't have and bought her gifts she didn't want. She hated the fact that because of this her mother wouldn't be able to pay the next few months' rent, and that she would probably need to ask her to use her student-loan money to keep from being evicted. She just wanted to run away.

With a box of tissue and a blanket, Maggie headed off to bed. It was her usual routine. She would cough and cry herself to sleep. However, sleep did not come. Once she hit the bed, her thoughts were too scrambled for her to be able to sleep. After an hour of tossing and turning, she decided to change something. She decided to change Christmas. She decided to make next year different.

She started a list. First of all, she was going to be healthy. Second, she needed to find out about love. She yearned for a love that felt good. Any guy she dated was lovely at first, but, eventually, they each ended up disappointed. She was tired of the pain. She wanted a love like Christmas stories talked about. She wasn't sure if she knew what love felt like, but she knew what it didn't feel like.

Maggie decided to investigate what was behind her struggles with Christmas. Why did she find it so difficult? What made her feel so frustrated and irritable at this time? What did love have to do with Christmas?

As she started her search about love, she first looked for books. After she read a bunch, she still wasn't sure, so she decided to talk to someone. Sid, a gentleman who lived down the street, came to mind. He had something special about him. She was touched by his kind way and his gentle spirit, even though he was very strong physically. That something special was something that she wanted, but she was unsure if it was love. She had a sense he might have some answers.

He went through life with a certain amount of grace, with a certain spark that she wanted in her life. She always felt warm and accepted around him. He showed such respect to his wife of thirty years, and when they were together, they seemed like a gentle wave in the ocean. They seemed to adore each other. Was that love? He showed this gentle respect and kindness to everyone, regardless of the person's age or status. Was that love? He walked gently on the earth, as if he were part of it, and had such reverence for nature and for all the animals. Was that love? If she could be like that, maybe she would be able to feel love.

She waited until the next time she saw him walking in the park. When she approached him, they started an easy conversation, and she joined his stride through the crunchy snow. There was a sense of comfort in their conversations, and he was very open to her questions.

Maggie waited for the right time and then staged a conversation about love, explaining her desire to learn from him. He was more than willing to answer her prepared questions. The conversation went something like this:

❄ ❄ ❄ ❄ ❄

Maggie: I have made a decision to have better Christmases from now on. I have had my last bad one. I know there has to be a better way. I am wondering about the love they talk about at Christmas. I am not thinking about romantic love or parents' love for their children. What is Christmas love about?

Sid: There are different kinds of love but the love you are talking about is the greatest of all love. It is not just a Christmas love, it is an everyday love. It means having good cheer and goodwill. It is simple but not easy.

I've seen you with your grandmother when she visits. You know the sweetness you seem to feel around her? She would play with you and you both would enjoy hot apple pie. The kind of love we're talking about is the kind of love she has for you. Her love never wears out. She loves you the same today as she did yesterday and as she will tomorrow. You do not have to earn it; it is just there. When I see you two together, there is a love that I can almost taste. I always feel when you two are together that I get some of it also.

Maggie: Is this the same as unconditional love?

Sid: Yes, it is. It is how we are born. This love helps us feel like we belong in the great plan of life. It is available to us, and it connects us. Sometimes we forget about it, especially as we are growing up. But it is the key. Sometimes in life we lose the key. This love is the key is to a better life.

Maggie: How does this love differ from romantic love?

Sid: Sometimes romantic love can change. It can have demands, conditions, and attachments. It can wear out.

Other people can take romantic love from us, and we can be devastated. The love we are talking about—unconditional love—cannot be taken away from us. It does not have demands, conditions, or attachments. It is the love Jesus talks about, as it is not defined by those who love you. With this kind of love, decisions are based on what is the most loving thing to do. It is about wishing each other well. Although it is nonsexual by nature, when you can love this way, you would be in a good position to love romantically.

Maggie: You mean I need this kind of love to have a relationship with a man?

Sid: It is the only kind of love that gives the relationship staying power. You do not need it to have a romantic relationship, but you do need it if you want a healthy one. It helps you love in a deeper, less needy way. It is there, even if the relationship ends, because you are able to wish the other person well. You are also able to wish yourself well.

Maggie: We were always taught that it is selfish to love ourselves. Is that true?

Sid: It is totally necessary to love yourself. You have to make sure you include yourself when you are extending love. One of the Ten Commandments tells us to "love your neighbor as yourself." I do not think you can love others if you are not in the business of loving yourself.

We need to remember that we were created lovely and beautiful. That is the key. Many people forget this, and then they start looking for love in other people, other things, and other places. They look everywhere because they forget the simple fact they are love. They are the thing they are looking for. Picture love, as a circle—loving God, loving yourself, and loving others. You have to be in the circle, or the circle will not be complete. It is by being in this circle that you live from love.

Maggie: What are some things that cause us to move away from our own love?

Sid: There are several things that cause us to move away from this kind of love. When we are young, sometimes we believe others when they call us names or put us down. If we believe them, we start to forget that we are perfect just the way we are. They might be jealous or just mean, but we do not know that. First, we give them power to hurt us; second, we give up on ourselves, which gives them even more power. They win twice, and we lose the key to our very own happiness.

Maggie: Can you give me an example?

Sid: Think of a child who loves to dance, but her parents make her sit quietly and watch television, or perhaps she is told she is too clumsy and will never be a dancer. That is quite a mild example, but it is nevertheless the beginning of losing the big key to life.

Maggie: What does creative goodwill have to do with love?

Sid: I guess the simplistic way to describe it is that it's the key to love. Creative goodwill is about loving yourself enough for you to be able to embrace and connect with others. It is about making room for others who might be different. It is about sharing what you have so that everyone has enough. Living with respect and kindness for all life is the key. But do not forget that you have to put yourself in the same equation.

Maggie: What does creative goodwill have to do with buying presents at Christmas?

Sid: Creative goodwill is a way of being, because it is about sharing what we have and extending best wishes to everyone in our world. It does not depend on Christmas, but it is a key to Christmas. The gifts that flow from this love will be simplistic by nature and given with the full intention of showing love. Even though there might be lovely ribbons and bows, there will be no strings attached. When there is this kind of love around, it feels a bit like magic dust.

Maggie: Magic dust! I like that. How do I get to have that? I am kind of visual. I can understand best if I get a picture of something.

Sid: You are an athlete and play lots of sports. The best example I have is curling. The center circle, which is called the button, has different rings around it. If you think of the button as yourself full of goodwill and love, then all that radiates from that button will be love. Let's say the rings represent your immediate family, your community, and the greater world community. If you radiate love from the button to each of these rings and beyond, you will be creating love and goodwill all around you. You could say that you'd have "Home Ice Advantage."

Maggie: How will I know if I have it?

Sid: You'll know you have it and when you don't. When you have it, that inner circle is childlike and full of light. You shine bright and sparkle with delight. You know you have it when your thoughts are of kindness and gentleness. When you know that everyone has value and that you have reverence for all things, you have it. When you lift others up, you have it, because you are being who you really are. If you spend time in nature and appreciate its wonder and can feel your connection to this wonder, you have it. When your eyes sparkle and you play and laugh easily, you have it.

Maggie: How do I know if I do not have it?

Sid: That is easy. If you let anger, resentment, or grudges enter your circle, you do not have it. If you have to win to feel good, you do not have it. If you are happy when something bad happens to someone, you do not have it. I guess you know because your light gets dimmer and you start to lose your sparkle.

Maggie: I have told you about my mother and how she acts at Christmas. She buys things she can't afford and she buys things we do not like. What does love have to do with that craziness?

Sid: Your mother is trying to show her love for you and others. She seems to be angry with your father for leaving her. I don't think she ever got over it. She might have forgotten her key. You don't show love the same way that she does, but that is just her way. You have not had the same experiences. You can't change her; you can only change yourself and your reactions. You have different options.

You could develop ways to love yourself more so you are not as affected by her behavior. You could develop some of your own Christmas customs that you would enjoy. You could learn to accept the loving intent behind your mother's gifts. The gift is only a portion of the exchange. Maybe you can think of all the ways that your mother shows you she loves you, and focus on that instead of the Christmas gifts. If you have love for yourself and love for your mother, what changes would you make?

Maggie: I think I might just run away. Do you have any suggestions?

Sid: One thing you can do is stop feeling obligated to do things that do not bring you joy. It is easy to get seduced by tradition and to lose track of you, your desires and requirements. I am sure you will find it rewarding if you take the time to think about you and what you really want. If you have looked after you, if you have given to yourself, you are in a better place to give to others. If you are happy, your heart can handle more. You might want to change things up a bit so your mom does not have the key to your Christmas. Maybe you could have the key instead.

Maggie: I have always wanted to go away for Christmas. Maybe go to visit my grandmother, or just take a trip. Someday I hope to settle down and have a family.

Sid: What is stopping you from going away for Christmas?

Maggie: I worry about Mom, and I couldn't leave her alone. She might be sad. I would feel very guilty.

Sid: To love properly, it is important to be in a good place yourself. It is vital to honor your body and your spirit. If you do not honor yourself, then you are blocking the love cycle. Your sadness, your despair, is a sign that you need some attention. Being a doormat is not a loving thing to do for yourself or anyone else. People-pleasing ways are not working for you. You could always ask your mother to join you.

Maggie: I don't think she would. She is quite stuck on doing Christmas her way.

Sid: At Christmastime, it can appear that giving in naturally proves our love, but in reality, the opposite is true. Real love opens us to new possibilities. We don't have to give in or give up. There is usually a win-win solution. The more real love we have, the less exhausted we become from giving. With it, we are better able to enjoy every day, especially Christmas.

Maggie: Do you have this special kind of love with your wife?

Sid: We did not always have it but through the years I would say we have developed it. We have something special for sure. She is very kind and supportive. She always wants good things for me. I guess you could say she is very well defined and confident in her spirit, so she is capable of love. She became my best friend. I was not as confident in the beginning, so I had a tendency to be jealous. That green monster got in the way. However, she was patient with me. She never changed. I did.

Maggie: What do you think is the single most important thing you did that helped you learn to love?

Sid: My wife was always my best friend. I became her best friend. I had to learn to trust. I had zing for her, but I needed to provide a place to let the zing grow. I learned to take her to that place so she could feel as safe as I did. I had some growing up to do. I became a better lover when I learned to love myself .It was almost magic. As I became more confident I could support her and she knew I had her back. What was important to her became important to me. As I took better care of myself I became less self-absorbed. It sounds backwards but it is the key to a higher love than I would have never known otherwise.

Maggie: I forgot what you told me about the love cycle. Do you mind telling me again?

Sid: No, I don't mind. It is always important for me to remember also. It is a constant choice. The cycle is a continuous flow that goes from loving God, to loving others, to loving you, and back again. Since no one is perfect, the love cycle is a lofty ideal. I think we can work toward it and redefine our position. We know when we are in the flow and when we are not. Where we often fall short in loving is in taking care of ourselves.

Maggie: How can I develop this kind of love?

Sid: You have to take very good care of yourself. You have to eat well, sleep well, and exercise. Sleep hygiene is the essential backdrop to everything. Some daily practices, such as silence, meditation, or prayer aid in the connection to the universal spirit. The heart that is clear of resentments and grudges loves best.

Maggie: If this kind of love is different from romantic love, is it possible to still have love stories?

Sid: For sure, they make the best kind of love stories.

Maggie: Can you tell me one?

Sid: The love story that comes to mind is about a remarkable man who has a high level of creative goodwill and consistently demonstrates it every day. He owns an auto shop where he fixes vehicles as well as people. He knows about equality and dignity, and he shares his gifts daily. His spirit is alive, and his heart is open.

I have been in his presence many times, and I have never seen him out of sorts in any way. He responds peacefully to others' needs. One night, a young couple from out of state was stranded on the highway because their vehicle had broken down. The police who stopped to help only knew of one person who would respond in the middle of the night.

When he got the call, in his usual manner, he got up, drove out to the highway, and brought the couple and their vehicle to his shop. He gave them a place to sleep in his home, and he showed them where the bacon, eggs, and coffee were so that they could have breakfast. Immediately, he went to work to repair their vehicle, finishing just in time to join them for breakfast in his kitchen.

The young couple was worried about the cost of the repairs, lodging, and breakfast. When they finally got enough courage to ask for the bill, the man just said, "Toodle-dee-doo," which was his way of saying "no charge." With him, it is just one love story after another, all day long. He is love itself.

Maggie: What a great story! It helps me understand this kind of love much better. If I begin to practice some of these suggestions, is it possible for me to have a different Christmas next year?

Sid: I guarantee it!

❄ ❄ ❄ ❄ ❄

On Maggie's return home, she thought about her conversation with Sid. She was so happy that she had spoken with him, as she felt much better. She stretched out on her bed, hopeful that her life was going to get better. As her thoughts drifted in and out, she he couldn't help but remember a story somewhat like the one Sid had told her. Maybe she had her own love story with a happy ending.

She thought about her high school coach. In an instant, she could recall him in detail. She could even see his whistle resting up against his gray shirt, and his pressed pants meeting his sneakers. Even though she hadn't seen him for a while, she could even envision him throwing the ball in the center to start the game.

She decided to write her story and give it to Sid next time she saw him.

For the Love of the Game

My high school coach shared his love of the game with so many people, in so many ways. He believed in each of us, and he focused on our character as a major part of the experience. Love ran through him to us as we spent hours in the gym developing skills in all areas of our lives. He never seemed to focus on the score or winning; he just seemed to magically provide us with high standings in our league.

Looking back, I think his enthusiasm, values, and desire to pass on this love provided the secret ingredient to much of our success.

He never yelled at us or put us down. Instead, he provided multiple opportunities for us to play so that we could have fun developing our skills. Every morning by seven thirty, he was in the gym so that we could start our day with play.

I was usually one of the early birds in the gym, playing before school, during lunchtime, and even after school. On the weekends, he was at the school, hosting games and tournaments, or taking us to similar events at other schools. I always looked forward to all the games.

Now I can understand and appreciate that the extra time he dedicated to us helped us develop confidence in ourselves. He knew that developing a value-based team was an important part of our success. He never played favorites; instead, he just kept pointing out each of our gifts.

Through this, we came to know each other's skills. I could easily throw the ball to my friend, as she was fast accurate and predictable. I was good at retrieving the ball. He made our strengths really clear. It was like his remarkable attitude spoke only to our cooperative nature, and so he brought out the best in each of us.

His love of the game and his desire for us to play well provided such a wonderful haven for a teenager. He taught us to value each other, the players on the other team, and ourselves. We learned the value of being prepared, and the importance of how to win and lose with the same dignity. It was never about the score or winning against all odds. Because of all this, we represented our school well, with both sportsmanship and skill. It was all about building, growing, and the love of the game. It is this love that has stayed with me, long after the scores faded.

Jesus Factor

"Love is patient and kind; love is not jealous or boastful; it is not arrogant or rude. Love does not insist on its own way; it is not irritable or resentful; it does not rejoice at wrong, but rejoices in the right. Love bears all things, believes all things, hopes all things, and endures all things" (1 Corinthians 13:4–7).

How to Get Your Jingle Back

Maggie felt better after learning more about love. Now she wanted to further her search so that she could discover more about joy. She did not know if she had ever experienced joy, but she knew she had never felt any joy at Christmas. First, she read a few books about joy, but she was still unsure how to incorporate it in her life. She decided to ask the local mailman, Francis, who was known for his sparkle. People often referred to him as "being full of joy." All she knew about him was that he seemed full of zest, always appeared to be in a good mood, and had a hearty laugh. He had been the mailman for years and seemed to have so much fun delivering the mail. He had a glint in his eye and seemed to take as much pleasure from seeing a new pup as he did an old friend. Mostly he could be remembered for humming a happy tune and always wearing a beautiful smile.

Maggie saw him on his route one day and asked if she could find out why he was so happy. She explained to him that she wanted more joy in her life. She was delighted when he agreed, and she prepared some questions to ask him (as she'd done with Sid) so that she could get the most from her time with him.

❄ ❄ ❄ ❄ ❄

Maggie: This might seem like a silly question. I need some help with getting more joy in my life. Can you tell me what joy is?

Francis: Joy is our sizzle and pop for life. It is who we are. We have it running through us all the time. We just forget sometimes. Love is the starter kit for joy. If you have love it is easy to have joy. When you think of building a house, love is the foundation and joy is the first floor. It is all around us and within us. Some call it the jingle we get when we are doing something we like.

Maggie: What is the difference between joy and happiness?

Francis: A lot of people ask me that, and it is a bit tricky to explain. I guess the best way to say it is that happiness is a result of something going well; we are happy to pass an exam or to hear from an old friend. Joy does not depend on things going well. It is more like waves of the ocean running through our body. We are not always aware of it, but it is always there, and it does not depend on things going well—it does not depend on anything.

Maggie: People talk about joy a lot. Why is it so important?

Francis: It is needed for a good life. It is a natural way to handle stress and grief. It helps us get over things, and it can be our best friend during tough times. It inspires us with sheer delight for being alive. You cannot be full of joy and have a pity party for long.

Maggie: Why do many people seem so joyless?

Francis: Fear. Sometimes people are afraid to experience joy, as they are afraid to lose it. People often confuse joy with pleasure. With pleasure, people get attached to material possessions. To feel joy, we need to focus inward and find ways to light our spirit spark. There are gifts of joy that only we can provide in the world. If fear keeps us from offering this joy, we not only rob joy from ourselves, we also rob others of the opportunity to experience our contribution.

Maggie: Is there just one kind of joy?

Francis: I know about three kinds of joy. The first kind of joy is the most obvious kind, the one that includes joyful experiences that we associate with positive things. This could be such things as enjoying a sunset, meeting with friends, or holding a baby. This kind of joy usually includes a sense of spontaneity, and the conditions related to it are positive.

Maggie: What is the second kind of joy?

Francis: The second kind of joy is deeper. I guess we could combine the second and third kind of joy. They are of linked together. This joy comes from letting go of grudges, anger, and all the negative things that cover up our joy. We experience that profound sense of joy after we have gotten over a hurt and then discover the gifts that were hidden in the grudge we'd been holding. It is like the silver lining in the cloud. Once we discover our gifts, we can then offer these gifts to the world. There is real joy that comes from the gifts found after sifting through the unpleasant things.

The biggest gift under all the unpleasantness is a delightful, magnificent, childlike spark full of all the joy we can imagine. This childlike part of us part holds the key to joy. This child remembers all the things we loved as a child and all the joy we tapped into so easily. When we offer these gifts to the world, we have a current of joy running through us. This spark is what is needed to sing our song or dance our dance.

Maggie: Can you give me an example?

Francis: I am thinking of a lady who has an amazing musical talent. She yearned to play the piano, but for many years, her musical talent remained hidden. After the death of her husband, she experienced a great deal of grief. While she was processing her grief, she discovered her voice. She now shares this with many people. It not only brings her great joy but it also brings others great joy. If she had not gone through this pain, her gift might still be buried.

Joy is not about things going smoothly. I have witnessed the joy of others even during very painful situations. One situation that comes to mind was a funeral for a child. Because of the situation, I thought this would be a very sad and challenging situation. I remember distinctly the warmth in the room as I entered the funeral home. It was even warmer than if I were attending a beautiful wedding. It was puzzling.

Many people had the special privilege of knowing this child, as their special talents were needed for her ongoing care. Knowing this child brought joy to her family, friends, and caregivers. All the joy was flowing from the pain of loss and from each person's special connection to this short life. It was as if joy ran through the pain.

Maggie: I learn best by visuals. Is there a chance you might have a visual to help me understand?

Francis: I am not sure if I can give you a picture, but since we both play tennis, maybe some examples from that can help. For me, there is a correlation between playing tennis and experiencing joy. Tennis takes me to my natural state of playfulness. In the middle of the racket is the sweet spot, and everything in life is better if we can serve life from this spot. The strings woven together can represent your gifts and mine. As I provide my gifts and you provide yours, the strings represent a community of joy from which I give what brings me joy and you give what brings you joy. They meet in the middle at the sweet spot, and we each give and receive joy from there. When we serve from joy we do not need the recognition of winning. When you serve joy you have already won. Hope that makes sense!

Maggie: It sure does make sense. What is the purpose of joy?

Francis: The purpose of joy is to help us live from our uniqueness, our special gifts, and to overcome our hurts. Joy adds zest to life, and it connects us to the thread that runs through life. Profound joy is seated it the middle of our wounds and our gifts. Although we can learn from others, we have to find joy for ourselves. It is so worth it.

Maggie: Can we create joy?

Francis: We cannot create joy, but we can create the conditions for it.

Maggie: What conditions do we need for joy to occur?

Francis: Some of the conditions we need to create joy are enthusiasm and childlike qualities. These are great for keeping our jingle going and for doing the things that keep our jingle going. Stay around people who have jingle. We also need courage to let go of our hurts. Joy grows when we notice the beauty around us and appreciate all that we have. You've probably noticed that many people who are full of joy have had very tough times.

Maggie: How do we start to connect to our joy?

Francis: We can best connect to our joy by becoming who we really are. We need to understand what unique gifts we bring to the table. What do we love to do? What makes us jingle?

Maggie: Can we do this on our own?

Francis: We are born with a name and certain gifts. Along the way, we might forget our identity. Trying to discover our giftedness in the middle of sadness or adversity can be tricky. It might be helpful to have someone else guide or assist us, but it is not necessary. Finding your joy and living from it is worth whatever it takes to find it.

Maggie: I am looking for some ideas to have more joy—or to create conditions for it, as you said. Can you help me with that?

Francis: First of all, think about what makes you jingle. Do you like to dance, sing, draw, or write? Do you love music and have a secret desire to play an instrument? Do you love to cook and find creating a meal delightfully satisfying? Do you love to chat with friends over a coffee and support them on their journey? What brought you joy when we were a child? Do you love to play a sport with a friend and share a cold drink afterward? Do you like to walk in the rain or have a nice long walk on the beach? If money were no object and time were not an issue, what would you love to do? Think back to your childhood, particularly of the times that you felt joy. Listen and you will be guided.

Maggie: How can I tell if I am disconnected from joy?

Francis: There are quite a few signs. If you are angry or anxious, or if you lack any sense of playfulness, you are off the joy track.

Maggie: How can I jingle a bit more?

Francis: Living with joy is living simply, with generosity, and gratitude, which are some of the highest universal principles.

To live simply is to know who you are and what really matters. It is about uncluttering our lives of unnecessary things, so we can have clarity and order.

Generosity is being able to freely share who we are and what we have with others. It is our understanding that we have needs, others have needs, and that we are able and willing to do what we can for them. If we know we have enough and are enough we can share. We feel safe enough to support others and sharing our gifts brings joy.

When you look at your life through eyes of appreciation, you transform your life into a natural state of joy.

Maggie: I've heard about Jingle Bell Disorder. How does developing joy help people with that?

Francis: Oh yes, JBD. People with JBD often feel they are not enough and do not have enough. When you fall into the trap of feeling that you do not have enough, you tend to hang on to things instead of giving. When you are afraid of not being enough, you may buy things to prove to yourself and others that you are enough. This is more about pleasure. Pleasure is fleeting. You may buy a new car and it gives you pleasure but that is not to be confused with joy. Joy brings clarity, simplicity, and fun to life.

When we have clarity, we can buy gifts that are appropriate for others, and we give them with the pure intention of expressing love to the recipient. A gift given from our true essence of joy can often provide a tickle in the belly of the receiver, simply because of its simplicity as well as its intent. A gift given from joy is appropriate any day—it does not have to be Christmas.

Maggie: Can you think of someone in your life that lives from joy?

Francis: When I think of a person in my life who demonstrates living in joy daily, I think of my late friend Viola. Mysterious and angelic by nature, she had joy running through her veins, regardless of what was going on in her life. Every time I saw her, she was cheerful, with a pure air about her. She had a deep, active faith and a strong prayer life, which seemed to help her maintain a warm and welcoming energy. For the many years I knew her, she appeared to have little attachment to material things. Her focus was on faith, helping others, and having fun.

She was trained in reflexology, and, as a result, she understood that each part of the foot represented a different part of the body. When I would visit, she would always treat my feet. Doing reflexology for others made her especially happy. She would evaluate your health by the condition of your feet, and then she would do what she knew how to do in order to initiate any necessary healing. She did this for me many times.

When she finished, she would bring me a cup of tea and a piece of pie, and then she would cover me with two warm baby blankets. She believed that they were the best for relaxing because of their satin edges and their size. Following these special treatments, I always had a deep, long, restful sleep.

In the morning, I would awaken to the smell of coffee, followed by a full breakfast in bed. Viola would be dancing with excitement, and she would always say, "I am all prayed up and ready to rip." We had an agreement that we would first do whatever was on her to-do list for the day.

The first stop was usually dropping off some food for a shut-in or for a birthday person. The second part of her list usually had a prayer focus, either going to a church service or visiting a church. She taught me a great deal about prayer. She taught me about praying for the people Who were in what she called the "vortex of the mind". She said to pray for them upon waking up in the morning.

During the fifteen years that I knew her, she remained ageless, as the silver locks on top of her head bounced over the rest of her long hair, which still maintained its youthful color. She attributed her agelessness in part to good nutrition, including cayenne pepper, lemons, garlic, and a daily cup of kombucha tea. She was always keen on fasting, as she felt it gave her more energy and a greater zest for life.

I didn't know how important fasting was for her until I stopped for a coffee one day when we were on our way to church. She became serious, which was a side of her that I didn't often see, and she let me know about the necessity of fasting before a church service. Fasting meant abstaining from food and drink, even coffee.

When we got to the church, we sat in our regular spot behind a lady with whom we always exchanged jokes. That day was different, though, as she seemed very serious.

She leaned over to Viola and whispered, "I think I am going to hell, as I am having sexual feelings about your friend."

She quickly responded, "Don't worry. She is going to hell too. She had a coffee before the service."

I especially remember a day when we went to an art gallery to see a display of work by a well-known artist. As we entered the gallery, an elderly gentleman approached us in a very rude and brusque manner, telling us to come back another day. Viola did not take his manner personally, nor did she back away from him. Instead, she reached into her pocket, brought out a pill, and asked him if he had a glass of water. With great disgust he shuffled off to fulfill her request.

When he returned with the water, she surprised him by giving the pill to him and saying, "You are far too stressed out. This pill is for you! Inside it is a friend for you. Put it in the water and you will see it grow. Anyone as grouchy as you are needs a friend."

As he watched his new friend begin to grow in the glass, she continued, "Tomorrow you and your friend need to take an extended holiday. You need to play and have some fun. I am sure when you return you will feel like a new man."

The man could not help but laugh as he witnessed his new friend forming. It wasn't long before we were having a cup of tea with him and going through the gallery. By the time we left, it was clear that her joyful approach with this man had completely changed his demeanor.

Viola was neither a victim nor a victor. She wasn't a bully or a doormat. She was always entirely herself: full of sunshine and spreading some light to everyone she met. She especially loved children. When she was with children, she would often squeal with delight. I realize now that what I loved most about her was her ability to be fully present and to have fun. To her, every day was so exciting.

Viola lived the spirit of Christmas every day. She lived close to the sacredness of life, and she laughed and loved easily.

Maggie: I love your story. I feel like I know Viola. I would love to be like her.

Francis: You just need to be like you. Once you become really sure of yourself and know what makes you tick, you will have a better understanding of what gifts you can offer the world. You have such a bright light inside you that when you are doing what brings you joy, you will light up the skies. This light will make you jingle and tingle. These gifts will show the world your unique sparkle and shine. Maybe if you think back on your life, you can think of some things that made you jingle.

Maggie: As a child, I was joyful because I was connected to nature. I so loved the trees and the butterflies. I could play outside for hours. I loved nature's paradise around me. On rainy days I loved going outside and feeling the rain run though my hair, and I loved the sound of the rain at night. I remember being so in tune with the movements and rhythms of the earth. I loved spending time in the woods and breathing in the scent of freshly cut hay.

As a teenager, I loved the feel and the smell of a basketball. My body longed to be moving and swaying with the ball. I so loved getting up early for school and playing a pickup basketball game before classes started. I dreamed of layups and rebounds all day during school.

I remember my math teacher had a sign on the wall under his

clock that said "Time passes. Will you?" Whenever he caught me daydreaming, he would point to the sign.

I loved books and my friends. I took great delight in life. It was like heaven on earth. I always felt like there was something great happening, something great had just happened, and something great was going to happen. My days started and ended with delight. I was very connected to nature, and I loved going to church.

As an adult, when I think of joy, I think of being still and feeling the warmth of my spirit. I derive such joy from children. I see their wonder and feel their passion. Their spirits are delightful, and my time with them is so precious. I think of times of play. I get the most pleasure when I include someone else in what I am doing, or when I really listen to a person going through a huge transition.

Some of my biggest joys come from supporting those who are sidelined. I feel joy when I think of joining my friend for chocolate pie before lunch and chatting about things like connectedness. I also think of long walks up the trail to the river and watching the ducks find their way. I think of playing different sports—skiing, tennis, curling, squash, basketball, and even golf—with a sense of pure gratitude that I am able to be there. I also think of the delight, calm, peace, and connectedness I feel while having fish dinner with my brothers on Friday night.

There is joy in knowing that we humans are connected, and in inspiring others to jingle. I experience more joy when I embrace my day with gratitude for everything. Keeping close to my spirit by playing and praying seems to give me the joy rights of my childlike innocence.

Francis: That was amazing! It was like a joy inventory. You have lots of joy to draw on as well, as you have a very active inner child. Hope you jingle more.

Maggie: Thanks for the chat. Do you think if I put more jingle in my life that I might have a better Christmas next year?

Francis: I guarantee it!

Jesus Factor

"'Let the children come to me, do not hinder them; for to such belongs the kingdom of God. Truly I say to you, whoever does not receive the kingdom of God like a child shall not enter it.' And he took them in his arms and blessed them, laying his hands upon them" (Mark 10:14–16).

Peace: No Assembly Required

Maggie continued her search for a better understanding of Christmas. Now that she had a clearer understanding of love and joy, she made up her mind to explore the idea of peace. Peace had always eluded her. Peace seemed like chasing a butterfly in the forest. She often wished that she had peace on the inside, and also wished she knew how to create peace on the outside. Both thoughts were fleeting and confusing to her. All she knew for sure was that at Christmastime she had no peace on the inside or the outside. She wondered if it was even possible to really have peace at Christmas—or anytime of the year, for that matter.

Whom could she talk to who could help her understand?

Once again, she started her search by reading some books and chatting with her friends about peace. Her friends seemed bored by the topic. They didn't have peace, and it seemed fine with them to live without it. Their general lack of interest in a conversation about peace led her to believe that she was the only one who had crazy Christmases. The information she got about peace from the books seemed conflicting to her. Eventually, she decided to talk to her grandmother, who was the most peaceful person she knew. She always appeared to maintain a sense of calm regardless of what was going on, and she also seemed to be very active in her pursuits to level the playing field for everyone.

A few years before, Maggie had attended a ceremony where her grandmother was awarded a peace medallion. She was delighted to spend time with her grandmother, and she always felt a sense of relief whenever she was with her. This was because of her grandmother's warmth and accepting manner, and also because of the love that Sid had described.

Until now, it had never occurred to Maggie to ask her grandmother about peace and how she'd gotten the award.

Her grandmother, or Granny C, as Maggie called her, always prepared her favorite snacks as well as a cozy nest for her well in advance of her arrival. This visit was different. For sure, it was inviting with same predicted comfort, but it was also an opportunity for Maggie to gain some key insights into her essential family questions as well as to fundamental questions about life. This visit was different than a summer holiday with her grandmother.

She usually would take this chance to relax and soak up her grandmother's kindness. This time, Maggie prepared questions as if she were going to interview any public figure, similar to what she had done before talking to Sid and Francis. Her grandmother graciously responded to her request for this knowledge. After their pizza lunch, they went into the formal living room. Their sitting in this room indicated the importance of both the conversation and Maggie's obvious passage into adulthood.

The two wingback chairs were the ideal spot for their conversation. Her grandmother's silver hair shone in the sunlight, and she held her well-groomed body gracefully in the chair. She appeared more pleased than nervous that Maggie had taken the time to travel the long distance to talk to her.

They engaged in their usual chatter, and then Maggie explained the nature of her questions and gave a copy of them to her grandmother to look over prior to the start of the discussion.

※ ※ ※ ※ ※

Maggie: I have some questions for you about peace. I have struggled so much with understanding peace, and when I thought of the most peaceful person I know, I thought of you. I am not sure what peace is, and I am not sure how to get it. Can you help me with that?

Granny C: I would love to help you understand this, as it would be the best gift I could ever give you. Peace is a bit difficult to describe. It is one of those things which, if you have it everyone knows it, and if you don't have it everyone knows it also. Peace is a state of serenity, which is total order. Peace is the acceptance of the fact that we are enough, we are loved, and we matter. When we are at peace, we live with integrity.

Peace is as close as our breath. Breath is constant, and it connects us to our calm center inside. However, we are not always aware of our breath. Life gets in the way. When we are at peace, we live in a calm relaxed way, as if our body is in harmony with heaven and earth. Peace is good for our health, and it is a great stress buster. It brings us clarity so that we can make better decisions. It is a little tricky to maintain our inner peace while living in a hectic world.

Maggie: Are there different kinds of peace?

Granny C: For sure, there are different kinds of peace, but they all come from the same source. There are the lighter kinds of peace that we experience when we are relaxed, such as a calm day at the beach. Our breath is slow and easy to trace. There is the peace in which our body and mind become settled and still. There is no turmoil. There are no worries. I feel this sometimes after a run or a good sleep.

And then there is a mystical peace that is always available. You can call it God if you like, but you young people have different names for God. This is the peace we all yearn for. It is the peace that provides us with a grace to meet the world. If we are connected to this peace, it helps us remember the boundless wonder of the universe. By being connected to this peace, I am connected to everything. I have the awareness that I am not better than the homeless person down the street. At the very center of our being, we all have this gift, and this makes each of us worthy of dignity and respect. Once I connect to this peace, I am capable of looking at others and seeing them as having equal value, equal worth, equal dignity. Once we connect to our inner peace, we automatically approach everyone with grace and dignity, regardless of race, culture, gender, ability, or religion. It guides us each to do our part, to help close the gap between the people who have a lot and the people who don't.

Maggie: What can we do with peace once we connect to it?

Granny C: The more we connect to this calm center inside, the more we have the capacity to help people remember their own divinity. Once we have order in our minds and hearts, we have peace. This peace cannot help but radiate out to the world, promoting the well-being of others.

One story about this that comes to mind is Santa making room for Rudolph. He made it possible not only for Rudolph to fit in but also to shine.

Maggie: What is one of the first things I could do to have more peace in my life?

Granny C: I think the best thing you can do is become a well-defined person. Know who you are, what you stand for, and what you are against. When you really know that you are loved, that you are worthy of love, and that you are enough, you will be capable of having peace. Once you become well defined and know your significance, you will have a better way of coping with the world around you. You will be able to keep calm in adversity. You will be more grounded and less likely to blow off in any direction.

Another thing to do to create the conditions for peace is to bring order to your life. It is essential to reconcile your inner conflicts. Reconciling with yourself and with others, as well as with God, will bring you to an inner state of calm. It will stop the war in your heart, your head, and your soul. Uncluttering your mind and heart is as essential as the air you breathe. When you make peace with your past you are more available in the moment.

This is easier said than done. Forgiveness is the main ingredient for peace, as it either lets you or someone else off the hook. It is a freedom of sorts. There may be someone that you need to make amends with, or there may be someone you want to reconnect with now that you can see with fresh eyes.

Maggie: That sounds like a lot of work. I have quite a war going on in my head, for sure. Is there a reason I should do all of this?

Granny C: We are meant to live in peace and bring the harmony and beauty of God to our surroundings. It is one of our soul's deepest desires. It is what we are longing for and yearning for the most. It is a longing we all have, and it is not dependent on our life circumstances.

We want peace in our hearts, in our homes, and in our world. It is not a constant, as we are not perfect. If we get some inner peace, we are sure to reflect that to the world around us. As we reconcile with ourselves, with others, and with God, we start the flow of peace in the world.

Maggie: How did you first learn about peace?

Granny C: My first idea of peace came to me as a very young child growing up on a farm. I hadn't even started school. I was the fifth of six children and still too young to assist with a great deal of physical labor. In the summertime, I was often selected to pick strawberries for the family's after-supper dessert. I had a favorite blue bowl with a white stripe, and a favorite berry patch.

As I look back, the outdoors was always so peaceful, with no one bothering me. I was never in a hurry. If I got hungry, I had a snack of berries; if I got tired, I took a nap. I remember once waking up to a small deer licking my face. I loved all of nature, and I felt so much a part of it. I was never far from the watchful eyes of the adults.

At any given moment, I would set my bowl down and chase a butterfly, or spend hours watching rabbits, grasshoppers, and bugs as they busily went about. I was a curious child, so fascinated by it all. This was paradise for a child of my makeup. Being in those red-carpeted berry patches remains some of my most treasured memories, not only for the total joy of it, but also for the paradise of peace I encountered.

It was during one of my berry-picking days that I got the sense that we are all connected, all joined somehow. I am not sure if this came as a true knowing, or if I had just spent so much time in the sun that my brain melted. At any rate, a permanent picture formed in my mind of a huge circular table where royalty, relatives both rich and poor, and people of different races and nationalities all sat as equals.

From this experience onward, I had an inner knowing that all people were of equal value. I somehow got the idea that my job—or our job, as humans—was to find a spot at the table for those people who had forgotten about the circle, who were never told about the circle, or who were outside the circle. I just had a sense that this was my purpose. It reminded me of what we had to do with the cattle on the farm: whenever one was lost, we had to find it and bring it back into the herd.

I do remember how excited I was when I rushed home to share my new idea. I remember my father standing by the stove when I arrived with my news. I am not sure if he was smoking his pipe, but probably not, as he usually sat in the rocking chair for that. I delivered my news as breathlessly as our neighbor would do years later when telling us about 911.

Like a fast-talking reporter, I explained how I had just discovered that the bachelors, who had a habit of drinking too much, were the same as the queen. I ventured on to say that people of all backgrounds, races, and religions were all the same. My father gave me a sideways glance, a look reserved for stopping people in their tracks. Looking back, I realize his cautionary approach was from his knowledge of the obvious pecking order in life that he had long observed. I have always been grateful that, even though he did not agree with my new idea, he never squashed my vision and dreams.

Since my time as a child in the berry patch, this picture has been so very clear to me, and it has been significant in how I relate to the world. Everyone seated around this universal table in my mind's eye put into the circle what they had and took from the circle what they needed. It was such a perfect picture, and the feeling I derived from it continues to this day. I can only describe it as "total everything" or "total peace." I felt part of everything and everyone; I belonged, and everyone else belonged too. In this circle, everyone appeared loving, joyful, and connected. When I revisit this childhood image, I feel harmony and peace.

Maggie: Did your concept of peace just come about from that realization?

Granny C: No. Although I knew that we were all connected, as a child, I did not think of this as being peace. I thought about peace as something else. I was sure it was an action, something you did, as well as something you were supposed to be doing. Although I knew the concept of equality and based many decisions on this, the world around me did not seem to operate in this way.

There was always the pecking order, with the influence and power that some people had over others. I tried joining groups consisting of people who felt ostracized and who experienced not being at the table. But even with good intentions, I often found I was not effective in bringing about any change, whether because of my own issues, policy issues, or other external resistant issues that I did not understand.

Maggie: Did you experience peace from doing those things?

Granny C: Unfortunately, no. I did not feel peaceful, nor was I building peace around me. None of the things I was doing brought me peace. In my daily life, I felt isolated, unappreciated, and tired. Many of my relationships were rocky. I was feeling angry, reactive, and resentful. Maybe I was trying too hard. Looking back, I can see I was doing the right things, but I was focused outside instead of inside. I was trying to promote peace when I did not have it. I started to rethink how I was living my life. At around the same time, a friend of mine asked me some hard questions during what he called a "working breakfast."

Maggie: What is a working breakfast?

Granny C: To me, a working breakfast is when a good friend takes you out early in the day and provides you with some very valuable feedback. These kinds of friends are special people who value who you are and want you to have a great life. They even pay for the breakfast, and after a couple coffees, they lead into what they want to tell you. It is always gentle and rewarding. They are to be cherished for their honesty and courage, as they are actually doing peace work. I hope you have at least one friend like this in your lifetime.

Maggie: What kind of feedback did your friend give you?

Granny C: At this working breakfast, I was reminded that I knew the equal value of everyone, but that somehow I had removed myself from the table. It was like an awakening to me that I had indeed taken myself out of the equality equation. I was still advocating for others, but I was forgetting myself. I had put myself on the sidelines, and I had forgotten that I too was an equally loved and worthy child of God.

My outside was not matching my inside. I had to relearn a way of life with me in the circle. I had to start the hard old road of reconciling with myself, with others, and with God. I carried a great many resentments, and I had some amends to make. I was promoting peace but not from a peaceful place.

Maggie: Was this difficult feedback to hear?

Granny C: It was at first. I initially resisted hearing what my friend had to say, even though I was yearning for peace. I resisted meditating or focusing inward. I was more comfortable being action oriented and outside focused. It took all the confidence that only a girl from the country could have, and I used it to start the process of going within. I wanted to run away from anything very quiet and still.

I was more of a rebel, and I wanted to create peace from that. An example of my outward-focused rebellion happened after my family moved from the farm to a nearby town. I was quite active and outspoken for the underdog. I thought I was doing peace work, but there was nothing peaceful about it. I just managed to tick off a great number of people.

Maggie: What were the hardest things you had to learn about peace?

Granny C: First, I had to unlearn much of what I had been starting to believe about myself. It is so much easier to learn than to unlearn! I had to learn how to create a spot of peace and calm inside. It was difficult for me to shift some of my outside focus to becoming still and spending more time in silence. But this is what is necessary in order to connect with and nourish this part of ourselves. I had to clean up some emotional baggage, and forgive many things and many people.

I had to clean up the home plate, just like an umpire does, so that I could step up to bat for myself as well as others. The hardest thing for me was learning to like my own company. I started developing the skills to better express my emotions and to stand up for my own dignity. Most of all, I had to sit still and then sit still some more. I found this stillness and silence difficult, but it was necessary for me to cultivate and maintain them so that I could live from peace instead of trying to "do peace." I had to learn to just "be".

Maggie: Is that what you mean when you say you live from peace?

Granny C: Peace to me seems like a cycle. The calmer I get on the inside, the more peace I have to extend to the world. And then it seems like the outside peace is reflected back to me, and I grow even calmer inside. The calmer I get on the inside, the more connected I am with everyone and the more present I am to everyone. This journey for me is not yet complete, but I now have a better sense of living more peacefully.

Maggie: What has been your biggest lesson from developing your peaceful ways?

Granny C: I am not sure what my biggest lesson is, but I know what helps me be more peaceful. For instance, if I am feeling upset, I stop and take some time to reflect before I respond. This has been so helpful to me, because I used to take things personally and react from the hurt.

I now know that many of these things were not intended to hurt me. Now when I get calm and thoughtful before I respond, I save others and myself a lot of grief. This frees up much more time for me to play and enjoy life. Actually, I make sure I play and pray every day. It keeps the stress away, or at least it makes it more manageable.

Maggie: I am still a bit puzzled about living from inside. What does that mean?

Granny C: That always confused me too. I have come to realize over time that it is a way of being that is in harmony with respecting yourself first so that you have more to give to others. If my life is not peaceful, I have little to use to assist others. I had to bring order into my life and integrate that into my way of being. For me, this helped build a calm center inside me. From there, I became more grounded. I do not take off madly in all directions. I wait and listen. There is a still voice that I listen to, and that makes all the difference. This calm center is a good way to deal with everyday things. From this calm center, I move into my life. Before I can even contemplate world-peace activities, I need to have some sense of peace within. I do not think I can give away what I do not have.

Maggie: Is it possible to create world peace without inside peace?

Granny C: I think not, but I am not a theologian. It didn't work for me. I have found that if I don't have it, I can't offer it to others. I have known many people who try to work on world peace, and they may even appear to be doing a great job, but their home base may be in chaos. What I think is best is to have a peaceful center and then move this calmness out to the people close to you, and then to your community, and, eventually, to the world stage. I didn't always think that.

Maggie: What does having personal peace allow you to do?

Granny C: Personal peace helps me be who I am, totally. It gives me my spot at the table of the universe. It helps me know that I am a child of God. I am open to receiving the necessary tools that I require to help level the playing field for others in need. It's like what John Lennon sang in "Imagine." Living from peace helps me develop a kinder, softer heart. If I listen from this spot I am guided what to do.

Maggie: What does peace have to do with our hearts?

Granny C: Peace is about opening our heart to help promote the well-being of others. When I am functioning from peace, I have confidence that I shall be supported and loved. This helps me avoid feeling scared and needy. When our hearts are open, love can flow freely to others. This helps us provide children with the tools they need to develop good self-esteem and become well defined. This will also help them know their own goodness. It is about knowing that all people have the right not only to have their basic needs met, but also to have the opportunity to live a fulfilled, peaceful life.

Peace is about opening our minds to universal truths. That means knowing that we are all accepted and loved by God. It means knowing that everything we do matters—our thoughts, our feelings, our words, and our deeds. When we know we are all accepted and loved by God, it makes it easier to see ourselves in others. When we walk the path of love, we are close to peace.

Maggie: What do you think peace looks like?

Granny C: For me, peace is more a way of being than a picture although the image of the circular universal table is still very strong in my mind, I now think of peace as way of being. It still consists of the same concepts as the universal table. Such things as inclusion, equality, respect, wholeness, justice, hope, caring, calmness, cooperation, and compassion are universal elements demonstrated as this way on being. You cannot have peace without them.

It does not include being judgmental, being jealous, being afraid, being angry, being a doormat, living in emotional turmoil or chronic chaos, feeling separate, or being a victim. When I started to develop a more peaceful approach to life, I had many things to unlearn in order to make the paradigm shift to a more realistic outlook on different situations. As I've said, it is so much easier to learn than to unlearn.

I have found some things helpful for cultivating peace within, such as sitting still, listening instead of arguing, speaking out against injustice and learning how to problem solve in order to facilitate win-win outcomes. Promoting peace is also important. It is about taking action in such things as decreasing family violence, and or participating in groups that advocate for people's rights. When I see a need and believe my gifts can make a difference, I am willing to help. Living this way gives me joy.

Maggie: How do you know if peace is inside or out?

Granny C: Peace is not just inside, and it is not just outside. Both happen at the same time. It is a bit like a rocking horse: it moves back and forth, from the inside out. As you reconcile parts inside you, they seem to reflect in your outside world.

Maggie: I am a bit confused. If peace is like a rocking horse, what did you receive your peace award for?

Granny C: I received my peace award for promoting peace. Once I got my ducks all lined up and had order in my life, I saw the world differently. I was led to create employment for the homeless. I had so much fun working on that project that I did not have any idea I would get any public attention for it. It is hard to believe anyone would be recognized for having so much fun. I had so much joy from creating this project that I did not need public recognition.

Maggie: Did you ever think of refusing the award?

Granny C: No, not really, because the ceremony actually helps others understand the issues of the homeless. The award actually inspires others to help out.

Maggie: Would you consider peace a gift?

Granny C: Yes, it is a gift from God, but we must remember that it is a gift that needs to be unwrapped. It is not a passive gift. It takes some effort on our part to become well defined, to be still, to be guided, and to know our gifts. It is simple but not always easy. It can be a sense of knowing that we are all connected and equal on a soul level, but we may still be conflicted about voicing this knowledge if we feel that we will be compromised. It is not always easy to follow the still small voice inside us, as it might take us to places we fear to go. We might know how to respond with love, but we might be tired and so react with anger. To live peacefully is to live simply and to act inclusively, which is easier said than done. You really must be rested.

However, if we truly maintain an inner calm, it is easy to spend time with people who might be considered different from us. They may have special needs, or simply greater needs than we have; or they may find themselves marginalized for reasons unlike our own. We gain the gift of their humility and wonder. If we come from this inner calm, we will also be comfortable spending time with people who are doing well, the rich and the privileged. Our sense of peace gives us the gift of feeling comfortable and calm with anyone, because we have that gift to give. We feel our connectedness to all of life. It is in this sense that peace is a gift.

Maggie: Why do people of power not understand this? They would be in the position to change things and to promote peace.

Granny C: People of power and superiority often live with a fear of losing their position. When you were a child, did you play the game called King of the Hill? One child stood at the top of the hill as the powerful one. Sometimes another child could knock the king off the hill and take the position. Sometimes it would take the efforts of a group of children to dethrone the king.

In the adult world, people of power can be afraid of change, as it may lead to the loss of their power, and this fear can be a barrier to their peace. Power imbalances are not consistent with having peace, and they can lead to unnecessary struggles, conflict, and even violence. The gift of peace can only come to full fruition when all are welcomed and all have the opportunity for a full life.

Maggie: How can we share our gift of peace?

Granny C: We can share our gift of peace by maintaining our calm center. This is not as easy as it sounds. We need to give from this calmness, so we also need to be knowledgeable enough to give meaningfully and generously. When we discern our own gifts, we give without hurting ourselves. People in need deserve to have their basic needs met. I was always shocked when I worked for a local charity where some people would drop off rags for the poor to wear. The poor do not want to wear rags. They have the same need for dignity that everyone else has. They have the same need to belong that everyone else has. The poor are people first. A heart at peace knows we are all connected.

When I realize we are all connected, I don't have such a strong desire to prove myself. I am able to meet heart to heart with others, to support them, or, perhaps, to remember their wonder. Sometimes others have to believe in us, to really see us, before we can believe in ourselves. We can pass on the chance to gossip, we can listen instead of judge, and we can learn to accept life as it is.

Once the war is over in our heads and we are at peace, we can bring peace with us wherever we go each day.

Maggie: What does peace have to do with Christmas?

Granny C: Celebrating Christmas can be a particularly challenging time, as it magnifies all that is going on with us. The extra pressures and expectations at Christmastime can rob us of our calmness.

At Christmas peace can be as elusive as the gifts on Santa's sleigh. It is a time that can bring up unresolved resentments, bad memories, and dysfunctional relatives, not to mention financial problems. This can cause so much stress. When I did not have inner peace I found it very difficult to celebrate. We can only truly celebrate from our calm inner place; it is from there that we radiate peace. It is essential to be in the business of connecting to our own peace. It might not be perfect, but we can make some positive changes by first being willing to face our fears and then asking for divine assistance. Christmas is the perfect time to remember and celebrate our divine gift of peace. It is a perfect time to be motivated by love. It is a perfect time to cultivate joy. If we are motivated by love, live our joy, and create peace, we are living heaven on earth.

Maggie: Thank you, Granny. What would you like for me to remember about peace?

Granny C: That you don't need a stamp of approval from anyone but yourself. Create and cultivate your calm center inside, and live from there. Take real good care of *you,* and honor yourself so that you can do a little kindness every day. Become very well defined as a person, and then you will neither be a pushover or a person who needs to feel superior.

Never treat anyone with disrespect, and never accept disrespect from anyone. Become a lifter of spirits. Keep all your dealings fair, and get on the other side of what your heart longs to do. Listen with your spirit ear, and you will be guided for the rest. Peace is like a golf game: after you have love and joy, it is just a chip and a putt away.

Maggie: Thank you so much. I think you have given me the greatest gift of all. If I develop more peace inside me, do you think I will have a better Christmas next year?

Granny C: I guarantee it.

Jesus Factor

"Peace I leave with you; my peace I give you. I do not give to you as the world gives. Do not let your hearts be troubled and do not be afraid."*(John 14:27)*

"Do not be anxious about anything, but in everything, by prayer and petition, with thanksgiving, present your requests to God. And the peace of God, which transcends all understanding, will guard your hearts and your minds in Christ Jesus." (Philippians 4:6-7)

[AUTHOR'S NOTE: "Maggie's Search for Christmas" reflects my conversations with Rev. Dr. N. Whitney, Richard Boileau, and Sister E. McCloskey.]

Part 3
Closing

Jingle Bell Order (JBO)

We have finally arrived at Jingle Bell Order (JBO) in which we now know how to be in touch with the sacred while living our daily lives.

Order provides us with a sense of comfort and safety and becomes an essential building block to a peaceful life. Having order in our lives requires daily effort and discipline. Order gives us the necessary sense that we are worth being cared about, and because of this, it is worth the effort it takes to continue cultivating that order. When we have things in order, we know we have supported and cared about ourselves. Bringing order to our lives saves us time and frees us up to do more worthwhile things. It also provides more time to relax, to listen, and, most especially, to connect with the divine.

This link to the divine unites us with our spiritual nature that helps us to understand how best to use our unique gifts. Tasks such as hanging the clothes in the closets, washing the dishes, and organizing our living environment may seem to be a waste of time, as they are only mundane chores. But the benefits of being orderly provide us with the opportunity to connect to new possibilities as well as other things that are orderly, all of which are divine.

All of creation has order, so to put order into life provides a backdrop for being connected to the natural sacred rhythms of the universe. Order provides connection to all that is true and good. When you walk in the forest and breathe the air, there is a mystical element to the order of nature. Order connects to higher truths and the flow of life.

When we have order, we have more space in our lives, and this creates more room for joy and harmony. After years of disorder, I got a new wallet with separate compartments for different things. It is so amazing to experience how much more enjoyable it is just to go out now. I instantly know where to find my keys, bank card, coupons, or anything that I need. Having my purse in an orderly state not only saves me time, but also gives me such a feeling of peace. I think it saves me at least ten anxiety attacks a week!

A few years ago, I volunteered for an organization that was very well organized. Not only was the office very clean, but everything also had its place and was consistently ordered. For instance, everyone knew where the scissors were, and it seemed effortless to keep them in the same place. In this orderly but busy environment, it was easy to get a great deal of work accomplished quickly.

Order transforms chaos. For example, once a room has been cleaned and things put in their place, there is a sense of satisfaction as well as a sense of peace that all is well. It is the same with order within us: as we become more congruent and aligned to the natural order, we have a sense of peace.

JBO is created by first developing order in our lives daily. Once we understand the value that comes from having order in our daily lives, we can use this foundation to help us establish order at Christmastime, when everything is magnified. It is then we can order up more jingle.

Jesus Factor

"… all things should be done decently and in order" (1 Corinthians 14:40).

Wrapping It Up

If holidays are difficult for you and you feel blue, shift to what makes you jingle.

As we complete the exploratory journey from JBD to JBO, it becomes apparent that Christmas can be different, even better, this year. This journey weaves through our perceptions, our reality, and our values. Hopefully, this process helps us close the gap on what we each perceive as our ideal Christmas and the actual Christmas we each experience.

During this process we have explored various elements and aspects of our lives that affect how we celebrate Christmas. We have also delved into different ideas and resolutions to ponder and consider incorporating into our everyday lives. As we explore these concepts, we gain more insight into how we can improve our connection to our own hearts, which will then enable us to have a solid foundation for celebrating Christmas well.

This process of preparing for our ideal Christmas could be compared to preparing to run a marathon. A person cannot wait until the week before the race and then hurry and scurry to prepare for a successful marathon on race day. To be successful the runner must have a daily plan many months prior to the race, preparing body, mind, and spirit for the challenge ahead. Once we put such a long-term plan in place on a daily basis, we will be better prepared to celebrate our ideal Christmas.

People with JBD

People with JBD often have the blues
Which resembles the flu.
Christmas does not measure up
Because of an empty cup.
However, you can let go of having to do
What makes you feel blue.
Instead, you can see what still serves you

So you can bust the blues.
Maybe find another way
To say what you want to say
In a sensible loving sort of way.
Try to make this season about who you are
And become your own shining star.
Add more tingle
And show us your jingle.

    Some questions, such as who are we, what matters most to us, and how much is enough, may linger with us long after we have read this book, and they may remain questions for us to examine on occasion. It is my belief that once we have a clear understanding of who we are, what we value, it will be more difficult to be caught in the traps of people pleasing and overdoing. Even though the celebration of Christmas has become more secular over time, it is the underlying spirit from the heart that is important.

    It is ironic that the stress, the divisions, and the conflicts that are magnified at Christmastime can be the backdrop for the change required to build a Christmas heart. By discovering ways to celebrate our creator, we can find the tools for building this sacred heart. As we learn to live from the center of this heart every day, we can develop habits that become more automatic. Life can become clearer and more meaningful when we learn to live from this heart full of peace, love, and joy. Living from this center, we are open to celebrate unity and freedom so that our very lives become a manifestation of this heart. It can become a way of life, and then, when Christmas comes, the ways of our heart full of love are magnified—so much so that we light the whole sky. We can finally love ourselves and extend our love to the world. We can live a full circle of love: love of God, love of self, and love of others.

    Christ, whose birthday we celebrate on Christmas Day, provides us with a great model of how to live a good life, a life about justice, compassion, and unconditional love for all. He taught us to see beauty and worth in everyone, including those who are marginalized by society. Most of all, He taught us about accepting ourselves, as well as those around us, without judgment or demands. Throughout the journey we have taken together in this book, we have looked at ways that can help us to move toward these ideals in our lives. By building this magnanimous heart and living from it, we can experience an expanded version of God that values all humans regardless of race, religion, class, or abilities.

Fox and Owl

Fox: I am worried about Squirrel. He is going madly in all directions. I am afraid he is going to pass out. What is wrong with him?
Owl: It is Christmas.
Fox: Christmas! What is he looking for?
Owl: He is looking for happiness.
Fox: Why doesn't he just take a nap or hang out with us?
Owl: He forgot.
Fox: He forgot happiness is an inside job.

Thank you for joining me in this learning process. I sincerely hope this has been a positive and nurturing learning experience for you. I especially hope that you have integrated more fun and lightheartedness into your days and that you remember to "play a bit every day—it keeps the stress away." When you live life connected to your jingle you will lift and shift the world around you to one love, joy and peace. When you operate from this center you will have created heaven on earth. Christmas will be a day to celebrate and remember; You are a gift. Your gifts matter. Your jingle will make you irresistible under the mistletoe.

Jesus Factor

"This is my commandment, that you love one another as I have loved you. (John 15:12)

To Jingle Bell Order
From Jingle Bell Disorder
Closing the Gaps
★

ANXIOUS CALM
ANGRY GRATEFUL
STRESS HARMONY
HARRIED VIBRANT
TIRED CHARITABLE
REACTING RESPONDING
OVERWHELMED RELAXED
THE DARKNESS THE LIGHT
SHUTTING DOWN OPENING UP
OVEREATING HEALTHY NUTRITION
NO TIME TO ENJOY PERFECT IMAGES
COMPLAINING EMOTIONAL HONESTY
WORRIED ABOUT MONEY GENEROUS
FEELING LONELY FEELING CONNECTED
MELTDOWN STATUS ORDERLY AND FUN
FOCUSING ON SELF FOCUSING ON GOOD FOR ALL
DISLIKING MALL SONGS ENJOYING CHOIR SINGING
RELUCTANTLY SAYING "YES" EAGERLY SAYING "YES"
FOCUSING ON WHAT IS WRONG
FOCUSING ON WHAT IS RIGHT
11111
11111
11111

Bibliography

Brown, Michael. *The Presence Process.* Vancouver: Namaste Publishing, 2005.

Byrne, Rhonda. *The Secret: The Power.* New York: Atria Books, 2010.

Choquette, Sonia. *The Answer Is Simple: Love Yourself, Live Your Spirit.* Carlsbad, CA: Hay House, 2008..

Gattuso, Joan. *A Course in Love: Powerful Teachings on Love, Sex, and Personal Fulfillment.* An Francisco, Harper San Francisco, 1996.

Gibran, Kahil. *The Prophet.* Rev. ed. New York: Alfred A. Knopf, 1973.

Hawkins, David, MD, PhD. *Power vs. Force.* Carlsbad, CA: Hay House, 2002.

Hoff, Benjamin. *The Tao of Pooh.* Penguin Books, 1982 Trumpeter Boston and London 2007

Holy Bible, Revised Standard Version, Catholic Edition. London: Thomas Nelson & Sons Ltd., for the incorporated Catholic Truth Society, 1957.

Long, Jill Murphy. *Permission to Play.* Naperville, IL: Sourcebooks, 2003.

Maté, Gabor, MD. *In the Realm of Hungry Ghosts.* Toronto: Vintage, 2008.

Morinis, Alan. *The Jewish Spiritual Path of Mussar: Everyday Holiness. Boston, Massachusetts Random House Inc.* 2007

Mother Teresa. *Where There Is Love, There Is God.* Compiled and edited by Brian Kolodiejchuk, MC. New York: Doubleday, 2010.

Peterson, Eugene H. *The Jesus Way.* Grand Rapids, MI: William. B. Eerdmans Publishing Company, 2007

Vitale, Joe and Ihaleakala Hew Len, PhD. *Zero Limits.* Hoboken, NJ: John Wiley & Sons, 2007.

About the Author

Jean-Marie Denning is a personal empowerment facilitator that inspires others to live their best lives. She is a generalist by nature with a keen interest in matters of the heart and spirit. She captures moments and relays them through her writing as a way to encourage harmonic co-existence. She has written three other books: Three Lives, Once Was Enough and Building a Heart.

Printed in the United States
By Bookmasters